THE CROSS
BURNS BRIGHTLY

THE CROSS BURNS BRIGHTLY

A Hall-of-Famer Tackles Racism and Adversity to Help Troubled Boys

Mel Blount

with Cynthia Sterling

ZondervanPublishingHouse

Grand Rapids, Michigan

A Division of HarperCollinsPublishers

The Cross Burns Brightly
How a Hall-of-Famer Tackled Racism and Adversity
to Help Troubled Boys
Copyright © 1993 by Mel Blount
All rights reserved

Requests for information should be addressed to:
Zondervan Publishing House
Grand Rapids, Michigan 49530

Library of Congress Cataloging-in-Publication Data

Blount, Mel, 1948–
    The cross burns brightly : how a Hall of-Famer tackled racism and
adversity to help troubled boys / Mel Blount with Cynthia Sterling
        p. cm.
    ISBN 0-310-39600-X
    1. Blount, Mel, 1948–. 2. Mel Blount Youth Home (Vidalia, Ga.)
3. Mel Blount Youth Home (Claysville, Pa.) 4. Social work with juvenile
delinquents—Georgia—Vidalia. 5. Social work with juvenile delinquents—Pennsylvania—Claysville. 6. Football players—United States—
Biography. I. Sterling, Cynthia.
    II. Title.
    HV9106.V532M453
    362.7'4'092—dc20
    [B]   93–13098
                                                                      CIP

Edited by Mary McCormick
Cover photos by Kevin Gregory and Anthony Neste
Cover design by John M. Lucas
Interior photos by Pittsburgh Steelers (pp. 1, 4, 5, 6), Mel Blount Youth
Home (pp. 7, 8, 10, 11, 12, 13, 14), and Kevin Gregory (p. 16).

93 94 95 96 97 / BP / 10 9 8 7 6 5 4 3 2 1

This edition is printed on acid-free paper and meets the American
National Standards Institute Z39.48 standard.

This book is dedicated to the memory of my nephew, Marlon, who filled my heart with joy.

Co-Author's Dedication
To my husband, Tom: I love you.

White House Memo

T H E   P R E S I D E N T   salutes Mel Blount as the 524th Daily Point of Light. Daily Point of Light recognition is intended to call every individual, group, and organization in America to claim society's problems as their own by taking direct and consequential action; to identify, enlarge, and multiply successful initiatives, like the efforts of Mel Blount; and to discover, encourage, and develop new leaders in the community service, reflecting the President's conviction that "From now on in America, any definition of a successful life must include serving others."

President George Bush, 1991

Contents

Foreword

M E L I S A G O O D person who's genuinely interested in helping others, in being successful, and in serving God. It's about time that Mel agreed to do a book, because a lot of people don't expect Mel to be the way he is. Maybe it's because most people don't get beyond his football image.

Mel and I have been friends for a long time, and I know just about everything there is to know about him—the good and the not-so-good. As far as the kids at Mel's youth home are concerned, I can say without hesitation that Mel loves them and treats them right, and he's not dealing with your Sunday-school best. All the wonderful stuff Mel does is no surprise to me.

One of the first conversations Mel and I had when he joined the Steelers concerned how he was going to use the money he made playing football. His family farm was in some deep financial trouble, and he was going to get it out of debt. He did. He also told me that he was going to have a place where boys in trouble could come and find love and discipline.

Today, he has two youth homes: one on his family farm in Georgia and the other in Pennsylvania. He also vowed that he would become the best cornerback in football history. He has.

Probably the best way for me to convey what Mel is like—and show what the Pittsburgh Steelers of the '70s were about—is to share this story I told the day Mel was inducted into the Hall of Fame.

My brother, Art, Junior, was on the field working out a young kid who was coming into the draft—the "hotshot" everyone was talking about. That kid was always bragging about how fast he could run, how high he could jump, and all the other wonderful things he could do. After Art gave our new hotshot a hard workout, Art told the kid to shower up. The hallway leading to the dressing room had a white wall. On the floor you could always find pieces of blue chalk that the players used to mark their vertical jumps with. As the hotshot was walking down the hallway congratulating himself on how good he was, he picked up a piece of chalk, smeared it on his fingers, jumped, and marked his spot. After measuring it, he declared, "I am the best! The best! This is the highest anyone has jumped all year. Yeah, I'm the best!"

Mel, dressed in his street clothes—cowboy boots and hat, jeans, white shirt, and long riding coat—was going down the hallway and witnessed the kid's jump and self-praise. Mel colored his fingers blue, walked to where the kid was standing, and jumped straight into the air. That kid had to have seen that jump in slow motion. Mel went higher and higher. A couple of feet above the hotshot's mark, Mel touched the white wall.

"That," Mel said, staring the kid in the face, "is the Steeler mark."

Every team has a combination of perspectives, values, people, motives, and goals. Bringing it all together is not easy. Chuck Noll used to say, "You have to become a team that's better than the sum of the parts." Since a team is a unit comprised of individuals, leadership must be present, and it must involve the whole organization, from the administration to the equipment men. The players of the '70s had that type of leadership, and Mel was a very, very, important part of it.

10

Andy Russell and Joe Greene were the earliest leaders. Rocky Bleier was also among the first, and when he left to serve in the military, he became an inspiration to us all. Greene and Russell set the tone. They asked for greatness from the guys and let them know what was expected of them. Then came Mel and Terry Bradshaw. What a pair! Both were great from the standpoint of tremendous ability—one on offense, one on defense. Neither came to us ready-made. They needed a lot of work to become great players. The Steeler organization had the patience to allow those two to grow.

Franco Harris and Jack Ham came on, then Lynn Swann and Jack Lambert. The Steelers had their leaders; the foundation was laid. One thing is for sure: The Steelers of that time did what they were supposed to do. They were the greatest football team ever put together.

A lot of guys with us at the time could have gone the wrong way. They could have been disruptive and selfish, but Mel and his teammates always let it be known that they were there to play the game as a team and together be great. Mel is laying the same foundation for the boys at his homes.

My last impression of Mel can best be told with another story.

One day, Mel, by then an ex-Steeler, showed up at training camp wearing his warm-up clothes. I noticed him walking down the hill and waved to him. He walked over and stood beside me on the sideline. I looked at him, then at the guys practicing on the field.

"Listen, Mel," I said, "you better get out of here."

"Why?" he asked.

" 'Cause you're making those little kids look like they don't belong here. You're retired, and you look better than all of them."

Mel laughed. He thought I was kidding.

I wasn't.

Dan Rooney,
owner of the Pittsburgh Steelers

Acknowledgments

I HAVE CHOSEN to write this book as a testimony to God, to serve as a witness that, through Him, comes goodness and light. I did not choose this path but was chosen to walk it. I was made strong through adversity, renewed through faith, and saved by grace. As the Lord would have it, those associated with this project are all Christians with a strong need to be of service. My co-author, Cynthia Sterling, is an excellent writer who possesses extraordinary optimism. She has a rare ability to see into the real person. Thanks, Cindy.

Thanks also to the Lee Shore Literary Agency that assisted not only in the writing and selling of the book and movie but also in the work at the youth home.

Dan Rooney, Joe Gordon and the rest of the Steelers, past and present: You gave me more than a few lines of thanks in a book could ever express. Many years of continued success.

To the Pittsburgh fans who stood beside me as a rookie, cheered me on as a veteran, and shared in my glory when I was inducted into the Hall of Fame: my deepest gratitude. Your support saw me through and continues to see me through the bad times. People like you do not come any better.

To Carol Locket and the rest of those at the youth home

who share my vision: You are my strength. Never once have you failed me or the boys.

There have been many who have donated time and money to the home. Their names would fill every page of this book, so I am unable to list everyone. Please know that I do acknowledge each and every one of you and send a prayer of thanks to the Lord that His people are so generous.

Southern University was indeed instrumental in my success. May you always serve as an inspiration to those who pass through your doors.

My wife, TiAnda. When you married me, you married the youth home with its growing pains, its problems, its many troubled children. Your love has made me whole again.

To my children, Norris, Shuntel, Dedrick, and Tanisia: I'm proud of all of you.

Clint, my brother, thank you for your devotion to the boys. Toopie, you always believed in your little brother. I don't know of anyone who has ever trusted in me more than you have. Thanks, thanks, thanks, to all of my family.

Momma, I love you.

And Pa: I haven't forgotten.

Mel Blount

Prologue

WE CAN NEVER separate lives into neat little divisions. All of us are composed of our actions, deeds, and thoughts. When I think of Mel, I don't see just a football player, or the founder of a youth home, or a man of God. I see a person who is expressing his existence in a creative and loving manner. I see a man who is complete and whole.

Football cannot be separated into little parts, either. It is much more than just a game. It's an event that brings us a little closer, as family and friends gather around their television sets, fans arrive early at the stadium for tailgate parties, and the team's colors are proudly displayed in every storefront window.

I myself always make a special effort during football season to go back home so that I can sit in front of the television set with my dad to watch a few games. My interest in football, my observations of the game, and my ability to call a few good plays have convinced my father that he has taught me well.

We talk about more than football. We talk about the individuals that make up a team. My dad will point out second efforts, players' strengths, their ability to concentrate, their determination and their pride.

"The way a player plays the game is a direct reflection on his attitude toward life. Remember that." He makes that comment at some point during every game.

With that bit of football philosophy in mind, the game becomes a study of people, and those people become a reflection of our values. Which player do we choose as our hero? Which one do we want to emulate? Which one gives us hope? Which one makes us proud? Which one stirs us into action? Upon which player will we bestow fame?

If you ever watched Mel play football, it will come as no surprise to learn that he knows how to deal with adversity. When his life was threatened, when both the Ku Klux Klan and the local press tried to destroy his youth home, and when a lack of money threatened to close the home's doors, Mel would simply say, "This is God's work that I do. Nothing will stop it." Then he would calmly go about executing his next game plan.

Football stars are often seen as two-dimensional characters painted in primary colors. Perhaps some of them are. But Mel Blount is God's rainbow, giving a home to discarded children and starting them on an adventure that will forever change their lives.

Mel is a football star turned hero.

Cynthia Sterling

Chronology of Events

1948	Born April 10 in Vidalia, Georgia.
1962	Played football, basketball, and baseball and was on track team at Lyons High School.
1966	Received football scholarship to Southern University, Baton Rouge, Louisiana.
1967	Father, James Blount, dies.
1968	Named Al-Swac at Southern University.
1969	Named MVP at Southern University.
1969	Chosen Pro-Scout's All-American as both safety and cornerback.
1970	Drafted by Pittsburgh Steelers (third round; 53rd player).
1971	Rookie season; started nine games.
1972	Attained semi-regular status.
1973	Started every game.
1974	Played in Super Bowl IX against Minnesota Vikings, Steelers win.
1975	Led National Football League in interceptions (11); named National Football League's MVP; named All-Pro.
1975	Played in Super Bowl X against Dallas Cowboys. Steelers win.
1976	Voted MVP.
1976	Sues Coach Chuck Noll and Steeler organization for $5 million (suit dropped).

1977 Named All-Pro.

1978 Played in Super Bowl XIII against Dallas Cowboys. Steelers win again.

1979 Played in Super Bowl XIV against Los Angeles Rams. Steelers win.

1981 Named All-Pro.

1983 Retired from football with team record of 57 interceptions for 736 yards; recovered 13 fumbles, returning for two touchdowns; returned 36 kickoffs for 911 yards and played 200 games, missing only one.

1984 Appointed by NFL Commissioner Pete Rozelle to replace Buddy Young as NFL director of player relations.

1984 Founded Mel Blount Youth Home in Vidalia, Georgia.

1989 Inducted into NFL Hall of Fame in his first year of eligibility.

1989 Named spokesperson for Safe & Sound, a program for the prevention of child abuse.

1989 Began Mel Blount Youth Home in Claysville, Pennsylvania.

1989 Receives: Pittsburgh Man of the Year Award for community service; the Whitney M. Young, Jr. Service Award from the Boys Scouts of America; the NAACP Human Rights Award; the National Conference of Christians and Jews Peoplehood Award.

1990 KKK burns cross on youth-home property (Claysville, PA).

1991 Honored by President Bush as the 524th Point of Light.

1991 Receives temporary license for youth home in Claysville, PA.

1991 Selected by *U.S. News and World Report* as one of eight national heroes.

1992 The City of Pittsburgh celebrates Mel Blount Day (March 3).

1992 Receives Walter Camp Football Foundation Award.

1992   Receives permanent license for youth home
        in Claysville, PA.
1993   Inducted into the Hall of Fame for
        Caring Americans.

chapter one

Clearing the Way

As long as I can conceive of something better than myself, I cannot be easy unless I am striving to bring it into existence or clearing the way for it.

George Bernard Shaw

T H E   A I R   blew cold, crisp. Snow was in the forecast. We, the champions, were about to run onto the field where we would meet the cheers of thousands of fans. Thousands more were gathered in front of their television sets, waiting for us, their heroes, to strut proudly before the cameras. Finally we emerged on the playing field, dressed in our black-and-gold uniforms. The crowd jumped to its feet, and their cries seemed loud enough to stir the angels in heaven. We were the Steelers. We were a dynasty. We were the best.

• • •

Where does greatness come from, anyway? I have been asked that question many times. The answers I have given over the years have varied, undergoing stages of growth and change, just as I have. During the last few years, because of my struggle to establish my second home for wayward boys, I feel I have found the answer to that question, an answer that will remain unchanged throughout the rest of my life.

The answer is simply this: God is a great gardener. When He plants the seeds of greatness, He plants them within many of us. It's a tiny seed that He buries deep within the darkness of our being. One day, someone or something comes along and sheds a little light and gives that seed a drink of water. The seed begins to sprout tiny, fine roots. It is at that moment that the seedling meets with its mightiest enemy—fear. Because it is the only thing that can kill greatness, the seedling must fight fear. The battle between the two is fought daily. It is the conquering of fear that makes one great.

I have witnessed the destruction of greatness many times during my life. A man, an idea, a vision is crushed because fear conquered the heart. To live in fear is like not breathing in enough air to fill the lungs. You go through life choking, gasping, and wanting—needing—more.

I've always liked breathing deeply, and a man my size has some pretty big lungs to fill. Breathing deeply has its own set of problems, especially when you're young, because your breathing area has a tendency to extend itself into someone else's space. It is in those spaces, however, that the biggest lessons are learned.

Looking back on my "young" years with the Pittsburgh Steelers is not always a trip back into glory and fame. In fact, it had taken me a long time before I could talk about those early times with a smile on my face.

•   •   •

I remember when I first reported to training camp at Saint Vincent College. The coaches had us working out on the field most of the day, and it must have been pretty close to ninety degrees.

"Hey, Blount," one of the coaches called out, wiping away the sweat that was dripping from his face. "Does this remind you of the good old Georgia weather?"

"Yeah," I answered, "It feels like our winters."

My answer threw him off a little. I suppose he thought I was some smart-mouthed rookie, because he made me run the field five times more often than anyone else.

"Hope you're as quick-witted in reading plays," he said after I had finished my jog, "cause Sumner gets you next."

After a quick shower, we shuffled into a hot, stuffy classroom. We were all a little nervous about what would come next. We talked among ourselves about our first day and what it meant to us to be chosen to wear the black and gold.

After a few minutes, Charley Sumner, a defensive backfield coach, walked into the room and immediately drew some circles and arrows on the blackboard.

"Okay, Blount," he said, pointing his finger at me. "Identify."

"Identify?" I questioned, not quite sure what I was looking at.

"The formation, wiseguy," he said, obviously thinking I was joking with him. "Well, Blount?" he said, walking toward me. "Identify."

The room fell silent as the coach and the rookies realized that I was not joking. I could not identify the offensive formations that the coach had drawn on the blackboard.

"Never mind, Blount," the coach said, stepping away. "You'll learn."

I had played all four years at Southern University on a full scholarship, but the game I played was different from that of the pros. At Southern I relied on my natural ability and little else. The game plan was simple: I went out and covered somebody, anybody. That first day with the Steelers I learned that, if I wanted to stay with the pros, I had to learn to play *smart*.

The coach looked at Terry Bradshaw. "Okay, Bradshaw. Identify." Terry just stared at the blackboard. He had no more idea of what he should say than I did.

As it turned out, Terry and I were alike in many other

ways, too. We both had tons of raw talent, but we lacked the structure and discipline to express that talent properly. Fortunately, we had some mighty good coaches with the patience of Job to teach us.

Unfortunately, I did not have anyone to guide me through the next problem that surfaced. It happened the day I walked onto the playing field for my first professional game. I was experiencing a riot of emotions, all going through my head at once. I felt like a man who had rehearsed a speech a million times, then at the moment he was to speak—forgot everything he was going to say. Then I looked up to the stands and felt myself confronted by a new fear. I was lost in a sea of white faces. I looked to the coaches for support, but all I could see were their white faces.

I had been thrown into a white world, and I didn't know my place. I didn't know where I fitted. Or how to fit. Or even if I wanted to belong.

Suddenly, I understood how the early Christians must have felt as they faced the lions. I could only trust that God's grace would deliver me from the white lions.

It was then I decided that they did not see me as a person but only as an afternoon's entertainment. I didn't like the feelings I was experiencing. I wanted to pull those feelings out of me and stomp them into the ground before they had a chance to grow, but every time I looked into those faces, I saw "them" and I saw me.

Up until that day, I had lived in an all-black world. Vidalia, Georgia, where I grew up, had unspoken yet well-defined boundaries. We had our churches, they had theirs. We had our side of town, they had theirs. That's just the way it was, and we didn't fuss about it much.

I had found tremendous comfort and security in the black world of my youth. Life was simple. The centers of our lives were our farms and churches. We did not occupy ourselves in the pursuit of collecting things for show or worrying if some country club was going to accept us. We had God's land to plow, and we thanked Him for that wonderful gift even when the soil turned to dust and the plants withered in the heat.

Vidalia was a million light-years away, and I knew I could not go back home, even though I had considered doing just that a couple of times. I longed for the familiar— the comfort of the farm, the strength of my church.

My struggle with the black-and-white issue caused me to adopt a defiant attitude that nearly got me cut a few times during my rookie year. I had developed a severe case of open-mouth-insert-foot syndrome. It was so bad that the Pittsburgh media honored me by giving me the nickname of "Motormouth Mel." I was once likened to Old Faithful, which only stops spewing water to build up steam so that it can spew more water. I had more or less appointed myself the spokesman for just about everything.

At one point I was accused of giving myself the nickname of "Supe" (short for "super"). I don't remember if I gave myself that name or not, but back then I was one cocky young man and quite capable of labeling myself "super."

If only I had understood and applied a proverb in chapter 12, verse 18, to my own life: "A reckless tongue pierces like a sword, but the tongue of the wise brings healing," I would have spared myself and those around me a great deal of pain and trouble.

The hardest lesson I learned while I was with the Steelers came early in my career. I was praying with the pastor and a few other teammates before the 1974 AFC playoffs against the Raiders. We gave a short prayer for victory and thanked the Lord for the opportunity He had seen fit to bestow upon us. When we had finished praying, everyone except me and the pastor left the room. I remained kneeling on one knee, my head bowed.

Lord, I prayed in silence, *You have given me so much and I truly am grateful. But, Lord, I want more. I want to be more, give more. I want greatness. Please . . . please allow me greatness.*

"Mel," the pastor's voice broke through, "can I help you with something?"

"I'm troubled," I answered, raising my head. For a moment I studied his face. The combination of deep lines and the hint of sadness in his eyes betrayed him as a man who cared too much. His burdens, I was sure, far exceeded the prayers of a struggling football player. I hesitated to share my thoughts with him.

While I was reading his face, the pastor was reading my heart. He knelt down beside me, waited for a few moments, then spoke softly.

"Mel," he said, "we haven't much time. The game is just about to begin, so I'll make this short. When you ask the Lord for something, you must be certain that what you are asking for is something you truly want."

"I'm sure," I interrupted. "I'm absolutely positive."

"Then the Lord will send you what you need. Remember though, God is the tree and you are but a branch on that tree. It takes time for the branch to be made strong. A mighty branch drops many seeds to the ground, and it also supports other not-so-strong branches. Its job is not easy. There is also a danger in that strength. The strong branch might think that it is the tree."

I did not have time to reflect on the pastor's words but rushed out of the locker room and joined the rest of the Steelers on the sideline.

I was ready for this game. I had studied the films on the Raiders. I knew them, every one of them, their strengths and their weaknesses, but I knew my adversary the best. I was stronger and quicker than he was. I felt certain that he came into the game knowing this; after all, he had studied up on me, too.

His name was Cliff Branch. Although I did not see it for many years, Cliff was the "branch" through which God delivered, on more than one occasion, the answers to my prayers. The message came to me, not with a whisper, or a feeling, or a rainbow but with a thump to the top of my head. Back then, that was the only way to get my attention. It's a good thing I had a thick skull.

At first I played Cliff real tight. I could see in his eyes

that he feared me. He respected the fact that I was one player you didn't fool around with. Then, little by little, I gave him more and more room. I began to play my own game and challenge my own limits. Concentrating more on myself and what I was doing, I failed to keep an eye on Cliff.

While I was busy occupying myself with my own game, Cliff was playing good football. He watched as I dropped further back. I was, like that proverbial man, given just enough rope to hang myself. And Cliff knew that.

The game was going great, and I was feeling good. Then the football came sailing through the air, and Cliff pulled it down. I swear, for a moment, Cliff's face became magnified as a smile spread across his lips in slow motion. It was that smile, imaginary or not, that became frozen in my mind.

A flood of adrenaline rushed through my blood as Cliff headed toward the goal line. Then a feeling of doom overwhelmed me as I realized that I had given him too much room. Branch was getting by me and there was nothing I could do about it. My speed had been taken hostage by his finesse. I stood there, watching him slip by me for a 42-yard touchdown.

My teammates filed past me as though they were paying their last respects. Bradshaw paused for a moment, and at first I thought he was going to offer some words of comfort. Instead, he lightly tapped the side of my helmet, lowered his eyes, and walked away. Bradshaw had also experienced his share of humiliation, and I suppose he was feeling pretty bad for me.

"Bench that stupid nigger!" I heard a man's voice yell from the crowd. "Bench 'im! Bench 'im! Bench 'im!" Obviously, a Pittsburgh fan had made it to the Oakland stadium for the game.

Yeah, fellah, I thought, *if this job looks so easy, come down here and do it better.*

I joined the rest of the offense on the sidelines, where I was greeted by Coach Carson.

"Sit down," he said pointing to the bench. His voice lacked any emotion.

"Sorry, Coach," I offered as I took my seat.

After the offense did its job, I got up to go out on the field.

"Not you, Blount," Carson said.

"What are you talking about, Coach?" I said, not believing that I was being benched. "I'm needed out there."

He gave some last-minute instructions to the defense, then looked at me. "The bench needs you more," he answered. "Sit there and keep it warm."

I could feel my blood beginning to boil inside me. The longer I sat watching the game from the bench, the hotter I got. I was being humiliated in front of my fans, the team, the opposition, and most of America.

Carson ignored me for the rest of the game. He never bothered to say another word to me. I sat on the bench, feeling like some useless rookie who was about to be cut from the team.

Humiliation is a strange thing. It can lead a person to either humility or anger. I took the anger route.

Finally, the game was over. We had won, but the victory was not like the other victories I had shared with the Steelers. I was naturally happy that we had won, but I was too preoccupied with my own personal anguish to care much. I was not upset about letting the team down or not covering Branch as well as I should have. I was ticked off at Carson for benching me.

"Hey, Mel!" a reporter called out as I made my way to the locker room entrance. "Whaddya think of Coach Carson's decision to pull you out of the game?"

At first I was just going to forget about it and answer with a firm, "No comment," but the more I thought about it, the more I nurtured that anger, and the hot-blooded, young fool inside of me just could not let it go.

"Well," I answered, trying desperately to suppress any emotion that might betray my anger and cause me any further loss of dignity. "I didn't think a smart coach like

Coach Carson would do something like this in a champion-ship game. It could have turned out to be the worst thing he ever did."

"Are you saying Carson isn't very smart?" the reporter yelled, attracting the attention of everyone.

"No, I'm saying I just think he took too great a chance, one I don't think most coaches would have taken."

"So," said the reporter, trailing after me into the locker room. "You think most coaches are smarter than Carson?"

The room fell silent as both reporters and players waited for my answer. A few players shook their heads slightly, as if to warn me to keep my mouth shut.

"No," I answered, beginning to feel that I was on trial. *What is this guy*, I thought, *a local sports reporter or some Harvard lawyer?*

"Well, you said . . ." he began to explain.

"I know what I said. I'm just not sure what you heard." I bent over to look him in the eye. "What I'm saying is that Carson took a chance. Let's leave it at that."

"How did you feel about watching the game from the bench?" the reporter persisted, thrusting a microphone into my face.

"Listen, I should not have been there," I answered him, pushing away the microphone. Then I pulled the microphone back and stated very clearly and very slowly, "I only gave up three all year."

When the press reports came out, you'd have thought I stabbed a man to death. Carson understood. At least I remembered hoping that he did.

That was the turning point of my career and the beginning of the boy changing into a man. I promised myself that nobody would ever do that to me again. I was a football player and I would play the game, every game. I'd show Carson. And I did.

I studied harder, practiced harder, played harder than I ever had before. I focused more on the game and doing my job. I set my goals higher and laid down a plan that would help me achieve those goals. I became a believer in second efforts. The higher I got up that mountain of effort, the faster I ran.

Yes, I showed Carson, but he showed me more. He demonstrated to me what a truly smart coach he was. As time passed, my "show 'em" attitude changed. Thanks to the Rooneys, Chuck Noll, and some fine assistant coaches, I learned respect for the game and responsibility for the team. I alone was accountable for how I played or didn't play the game.

My physical strength, height, and swiftness had already made me a cut above the rest. God saw fit to give these gifts to me, and I had been repaying Him by blaming others when I fell short. Well, no more, I promised myself.

Somewhere along the line I began to realize that every mistake I made was an opportunity to learn. Instead of thinking about how many times I had been beaten, I decided to think about how many lessons I had learned. I began to find myself becoming a little bit wiser, and with that sense of wisdom I started to feel comfortable in my new environment.

Once again I belonged.

chapter two
The Vision

Vision: the art of seeing things invisible.
                                                  Jonathan Swift

P L A Y I N G   F O O T B A L L   with the Pittsburgh Steelers has been an honor that defies description. The impact that the game of football made on my life is like the force of the sun on a blossom. The Steeler organization offered me a training ground and an opportunity to refine my talents that helped mold me into the person I am today. The only thing they asked in return was that I do my job, a job that I loved.

These days I have more on my mind than how I played football. The glory years are gone for me, and I don't regret their passing. I left the game knowing that I had done my best and set a standard to which all cornerbacks would aspire. The adjustment after football came easy. I had simply left one life to enter another.

The Steelers did a good job of reminding all us players that football was only temporary. Chuck Noll put it best when he said, "One day, you'll have to get to your life's work."

I think everyone is born with his life's work already programmed into him. It sits next to the seed of greatness.

31

However, locating that program is like sitting down at a computer for the first time and not knowing how to turn it on.

Although I didn't recognize it at the time, my life's work began to surface when I was with the Steelers. We were playing the Dolphins in Miami. We had arrived a few days early, and I had a chance to walk around the city. That's when I spotted Trevor on the streets. He was one among the many thousands of kids that I call the shadow children, abandoned children caught between the worlds of light and darkness. A kind word, a little love can bring them into the light; pretending you don't see them forces them deeper into the darkness until they disappear altogether.

I'm not sure what overtook me, but, when I looked into Trevor's eyes, I saw a glimmer of my own future. I made arrangements with the authorities and gained custody of Trevor, who was about nine or ten years old.

I wasn't quite sure what I was going to do with him. I was on the road most of the time and in no position to be a father to another boy. When the Dolphins' game was over, I quietly left the locker room. I could hear Terry Bradshaw giving an analysis of the game to the reporters, and once or twice I heard my name being called out as I was asked for comments. The celebration of winning would go on without me. I walked out into the parking lot of the stadium where Trevor was waiting for me.

I can only imagine what was going through his mind as we walked to my rented car. Some six-foot-three, black, bald football player dressed in black and gold whom he had just met a few days ago was going to take him off the streets and whisk him away to a farm in Georgia. I am sure he didn't know whether this was a dream come true or a nightmare.

We arrived later that night in Vidalia and I introduced Trevor to my momma.

"Come here, boy," she said, with her arms wide. She gave him a hug, then looked up at me. "I guess this is the newest member of our family."

I nodded.

"Yes, ma'am," Trevor answered, tears in his eyes.

"No need to cry, boy," Momma whispered in his ear. "You're safe here."

"I know, ma'am," said Trevor, wiping away the tears that dripped down his face. "That's why I'm cryin'."

"God bless you, Momma," I said, kissing her on top of the head. "You raised us eleven kids and a few children besides, and you still have so much love to give."

"What's another boy around here?" she asked, getting up from her chair. "We have plenty of room and enough of everything to go around."

Trevor soon became just another part of our family. I had a hand in bringing him up, but it was my momma and my brother, Clint, who did most of the work.

One day Clint and I were talking at our family reunion about the difference we had made in Trevor's life. A frightened little boy was growing into a confident young man who was beginning to see that life is good. As we watched Trevor playing with our nieces and nephews, we felt inspired. It was as if the hand of God had touched us with a special gift.

"I'm wondering, Clint," I said, rubbing my bald head. "Do you think there's a way we can help more of these kids?"

"I'm sure there is, brother," Clint answered as he caught a football that came soaring his way. "But don't ask me what the answer is. Ask God."

"Well, God," I said out loud, "What's the answer?"

A few months later, the answer arrived by way of the town's sheriff.

"Hi there, Mel," he began. "I've been watching you on TV, and I am mighty impressed by how you play football. Most of the folks around here think that someday you're gonna be more famous than our onions. I think they may be right. Your daddy sure would have been proud of a son like you. Yeah, I can almost hear him now. 'Nah, Mel isn't any more special than the rest of my kids. God's gotta make some tall, fast people. Ain't nothin' too special about that.'"

I smiled. Sheriff Grover had been one of my dad's closest friends and my connecting link between the white and black communities of Vidalia. The sheriff was a respected authority in the white section of town. My dad, who was much like a tribal leader, held the same position of respect in our community.

The sheriff had mimicked my dad's voice so well that for a moment I saw him standing in front of me, looking as he did the day I left home to return to Southern University for my second semester. I knew our farm was going through some hard times, and I could tell from my dad's face that it was real serious this time. I was reluctant to return to school, knowing that the farm needed me.

Our Georgia farm is just about the most beautiful place in the world. My grandpa bought its 2200 acres a piece at a time. The story goes that the white folks at the time were not too concerned that a former slave was buying up so much land. They figured that Grandpa wasn't smart enough to manage that much property and would be forced to sell off his land during the years when the crops failed. But my grandpa never sold land; he just bought it. The only land he gave up was the land he donated for a church and a couple of graveyards, but he never sold land. To a farmer, the only things more important than land are his family and God.

After Grandpa died, the farm continued to produce, but then came several years in a row that the sun beat down too hot and the clouds were too stingy to give the dried-out soil a drink. My dad was forced to sell a few acres to pay off the loans that he had made to buy seed that never produced and to see the family through until another crop could be planted from more mortgaged seeds.

"Son," my dad said as he watched me toss my clothes into the suitcase. "I don't want you to be thinkin' about the farm while you're away at college. Just study hard and play your football proud. When the Lord gave you that scholarship, He meant for you to leave the farm. You ain't gonna be a farmer like me and your granddaddy. Rest your mind, Mel, God will see us through this."

"But Pa, I can't just leave you here like this." My heart was breaking as I watched him put up such a brave front for me.

"The farm will always be here waiting for you when it's time for you to come home," my dad said, turning away.

"Hey there, Mel," said the sheriff, interrupting my thoughts. "I got a proposition for you."

"I'm listening, Sheriff," I said, making myself comfortable on the hood of his car.

"I just picked up a local white boy for robbing Mr. Dan's grocery store. This kid ain't bad. He's just wayward and doesn't have anyone who cares to straighten him out. I was thinking that, since you took in the little guy from Florida, you might see your way clear to give this kid a hand, too. Dan has agreed to drop the charges and has offered to donate some food from time to time to help you out."

"Well, I don't know, Sheriff. Momma's not getting any younger and I'm home less and less." I paused for a few minutes. "Oh, what the heck! If he needs a place to stay, we can make room."

More and more "wayward boys" came, and before long, the money I was making playing football was not enough to keep the farm going and the kids housed, clothed and fed, plus take care of my own family and their needs.

My position was a good example of how much football players were getting back in the seventies and early eighties. I was coming off the best year I ever had. I was the NFL's Defensive MVP, the Steelers' MVP, and I led the league in interceptions. And my salary was less than $50,000. In 1976, I was MVP in the Pro Bowl and still making under $50,000. I had been asking for more money, and the Steelers promised that they would take care of me at the end of the season.

Before the 1977 season was about to begin, Jim Boston, the Steelers' contract negotiator, met with me in Louisiana. He offered me a $5,000 raise. The "benching incident" flashed through my mind. I could not believe I was hearing correctly and decided that he must be joking.

35

"Come on, Jim," I said when I realized that the offer was real. "There's no way I can accept that."

His answer was simple and to the point: "Take it or starve."

Take it or starve. I let those words roll around in my head for a second or two, then I understood that there was a big difference between where I thought I stood with the Steeler organization and where they had placed me.

I felt as if I was being used. My decision was simple. I had always known that football was a passing moment: I just never thought my moment would pass so quickly. But I knew I could survive without football, so I held out.

The contract dispute took an interesting twist that plagued me throughout my football career and beyond. While I was holding out, Chuck Noll was sued for two million dollars by George Atkinson of the Oakland Raiders for slander. The season before, Lynn Swann had been roughed up pretty badly by Atkinson, and Noll made some off-handed remark that Atkinson was a member of the "criminal element" that existed in the NFL.

At the court hearing, the lawyers for Atkinson showed Noll a clip of me slamming Cliff Branch, my messenger from God, to the ground. I had never had the reputation of being a dirty player, and my hit against Cliff Branch was intended to stop him, not injure him. When the lawyers asked Noll what he thought of me, he said I was also a member of that same criminal element.

I was already mad, and this made me furious, not only at Chuck Noll, but at the whole Steeler organization. I filed a suit against Noll and the Steelers for $5,000,000.

After my temper died down and I took a good look at things, I still did not like the fact that I had been labeled by my own coach as a criminal, but I realized that Noll was under a lot of pressure during the trial. Sometimes we all say things we don't really mean, or the words get twisted around and used against us.

I did then, and still do, see the Steelers' offer of $5,000 as a slap in the face. The black players were in a constant battle for their equal shares, both on and off the field. There were two pay scales: one for the white player and another for the black player. Even when it came to promotion and publicity, the black player did not get much. If two players were needed to deliver a speech at two separate functions, the white player always came up with the better one. He would go to the plush hotel, give his speech, and dine on steak and lobster. The black player would end up in an inner-city school auditorium, eating hot dogs.

Anyway, we never went to court, and the suit was dropped. I did not get $5,000,000, or even the $100,000 I was holding out for. Instead, Chuck Noll, the Steelers, and I went back to playing the game. We put our brief confrontation behind us.

One thing that I think came out of the whole lawsuit was that I won a new respect from Chuck Noll. He saw that I was willing to stick by my convictions. Some people still believe that Noll and I carry this incident with us as a grudge against each other, but that's not the case. We understand that we are both men of action, and men of action often clash.

By 1983, Clint had laid down a plan that he was certain would help us ease the money situation caused by taking in so many boys. "Look, Mel," Clint said, showing me a freshly painted sign. "We found a name for our youth home."

"The Mel Blount Youth Home for Wayward Boys," I read aloud. "No way, Clint, I can't agree to this." It had seemed to me that, when you're doing something good, just the doing was good enough. I didn't want that kind of publicity.

"Listen, Mel," Clint said firmly, "we need some help here or there won't be a home for these boys much longer. There are not many people who will give money to some black man who spends it on kids that look like they haven't got a future, but if Mel Blount is asking, well, they'll give."

He was right. I hate to say this, but a lot of people gave money only because they wanted to associate their names with mine. I guess I used them as much as they used me, because I took the money.

Since I was still on the road playing football back then, it was really Clint who was the major force behind the first home. For the most part, he still is. However, that's not the case with the youth home in Claysville, Pennsylvania, which is about fifty minutes from downtown Pittsburgh. I'm in full charge and completely responsible for everything that goes on there.

It had taken over a year to find a suitable site near Pittsburgh for this youth home, and my search was difficult in a lot of ways. I must have looked at a thousand farms. There were more than a few people who would not sell to a black man. None of them actually gave that as a reason, but you would be surprised how quickly a piece of land can find a buyer when Mel Blount expresses an interest in it. Maybe my color had nothing to do with it; maybe it was just me. I hear that I look pretty intimidating.

One day, I found a few hundred acres tucked away in a back forest. At first I had my doubts about it: To get there took thirty minutes on a dirt road that wound around one of those steep Pennsylvania hillsides. But the more I walked around, the more I was attracted to the isolation. I put my doubts aside and put some money down on the land. I had six weeks to come up with the rest.

By the beginning of the sixth week, I was still raising the money by selling off a few things I owned, so I met with the owner to explain the situation.

"I only need a few more weeks," I said, after finishing the lengthy story of how someday the land would become a home for boys. I felt that he understood where I was coming from because he listened intently to each and every word, nodding in agreement from time to time.

Then he looked me straight in the eye and said, "Nope."

There was not one bit of that answer that I did not understand. I had already guessed the answer to my next question, but I asked anyway.

"Do you think that you could see your way clear to giving me back my money so I can find another place?"

"Nope."

Things worked out, though. Soon after that little fiasco, I made a guest appearance on the Ann Devlin show, a local television talk program. After we got through the football glories, we started to talk about what I was doing at present. I told her I was looking to buy a farm to establish a home for boys, but I was not having much luck.

Before the show aired, I left for Hawaii, where I was being introduced at the halftime of the Pro Bowl with the new Hall of Fame class. Matt Onopiuk, an older gentleman who saw the show, arranged to have the Steelers get a message to me that he was willing to sell me his farm.

"I want $450,000 for it," Matt said right up front after we toured the farm. "Not a penny less than $450,000."

"Are you willing to arrange terms with me?" I asked, because at that moment the Mel Blount Youth Home, Inc., did not have a cent to its name.

"Sure thing, Mr. Blount," he said.

Right there I gave him $5000 of my own money. Another $95,000 was due when we signed the land contract. That was around February 1989. I had no idea where I was going to come up with $95,000, and I had not even begun to think about where the money was going to come from to meet the agreed-upon payment schedule. I just trusted.

Isn't it just like the Lord to put you in a position that has you momentarily questioning His decision-making process? Mr. Onopiuk's farm was a 240-acre spread in the middle of Washington County, a part of Pennsylvania that borders West Virginia. The farmhouse was a shambles, the barn was falling apart, and everywhere I looked, heaps of trash littered the ground.

Are you sure, Lord, that this is the place? I asked. I was not so much doubting Him as I was doubting my ability to transform this wreck into a home where people could actually live. Then I figured, if the Steelers could make a good football player out of me, I could, with God's help, make a home for the boys.

A few weeks passed and I was hustling to find money. Like a godsend, the owner of Mountaineer Park struck a deal with me to be a spokesman for the park and generously gave me a $200,000 bonus for signing up to work with him. I lent that money to the youth home, and we were off and running. That is, *I* was off and running, and my fast-paced lifestyle was about to catch up with me.

Raising money, losing money, spending time searching and having people not like you because you're black . . . none of these woes compared to the pain of a personal loss I had to face. I had been married to Leslie for nineteen years, and now my marriage was breaking up. I had always been able to make things work out in the past, but I could not save our marriage.

There were many reasons why we did not make it. I was not home much during most of our marriage, and when the traveling slowed down, Leslie and I discovered that we had built our lives separately from one another. It was as if we were both in the middle of the ocean, trying to communicate from our own separate islands. The louder we called to each other, the more the wind scattered our words. We stood by helplessly as our love drowned in the waves.

Looking back, I can see all the warning signs that I missed—the forgotten birthdays, the anniversaries spent apart, the missed phone calls. We had stopped sharing the little details of our days and eventually did not share the big things.

A marriage does not break up because of travel, football, or busy schedules, and I am not blaming those things. I have accepted the responsibility for my failure. Somewhere, both Leslie and I stopped working at our relationship.

I sat many evenings in the living room of that big, old, lonely farmhouse with only my failed marriage to keep me company. I reviewed every aspect of my marriage, searching for where I went wrong. I was beating myself up.

One day, I picked up the Bible and clasped it in my hands. "Lord," I prayed out loud. "I'm hurting all over. I lost my family, the most important thing in my life, and they are not coming back."

I cried for hours. Then I started to look at the good things: the loving, the caring, and the laughter of all those years. And there were my wonderful children: My spirit warmed at the mere thought of them. Leslie and I had indeed raised up a family filled with love. That was the one thing I could hold onto forever.

Then I realized that I was still a good person. I still liked myself. Most important, I realized that God forgives when we are truly repentant.

It was strange, because at that moment I swear I actually heard my dad's voice talking to me. "Don't forget the boy." Suddenly, my way was clear, and I was lifted out of my sense of failure. All that I could see before me was my vision of the youth home. There I stood, tears dried, Bible in hand, seeing the invisible.

chapter three
The Town Meeting

The recipe for perpetual ignorance is: Be satisfied with your opinions and content with your knowledge.

Elbert Hubbard

T H E   T I M E   for contemplation was over. I had seen my vision and I had gathered up the pieces of my life. I was ready to get back into the game.

It was just about dawn, and I decided I'd better be about my business. I knew there was a starting point to be found somewhere in the piles of junk on the farm property, but it took most of the day for me to find that point. I had an overwhelming job ahead of me. I could not help but think that Mr. Rooney and Chuck Noll had asked the same question about me: Where do I begin?

I headed back to the farmhouse and grabbed the Yellow Pages. Junk removal. As good a place to start as any.

"Hello. This is Mel Blount," I said, pouring a glass of grapefruit juice. "I'd like someone to come out to my farm and give me a few quotes on taking some trash away."

"Is this you, George?" a man's voice asked.

"No, this is Mel Blount," I said, taking a gulp of juice.

"Naw, really? The Mel Blount who played for the Steelers?"

I guess I was still able to impress a few people, because we made arrangements to meet that same afternoon. Henry, the man I talked to, waved from his pick-up truck as he wound his way up the hill to the farmhouse. He had brought George, his partner, along with him.

We talked a little football as the two men walked around the property, surveying the trash.

"You've got a mighty big mess here, Mr. Blount," Henry said, shaking his head.

"Fellahs, I appreciate you coming all the way out here," I replied, "but I got to be real straight with you. I don't have any money."

They both looked astonished. A football star without money? I explained the situation to them and shared with them my vision of the youth home. "I need to get things underway here. If you can lend me a hand, I can pay you in a couple of weeks."

It did not take Henry and George long to make a decision. Just as they had said they would, they arrived early the next morning with a crew of men.

The clean-up lasted for a good week, and I worked alongside the guys. We filled truck after truck with loads of debris.

"Hey, Mel," George called out one morning, holding up a discovery he had made among the trash. "Catch this one."

A worn, half-deflated football came sailing through the air. I had raised my hands to catch it when Henry came flying in front of me and picked it off.

The expression of joy that spread across his face was so pronounced that all of us began to laugh.

"I've always wanted to play with the pros," Henry said, smiling. "Now I have."

That was a happy day for me. The fellowship we shared is how things are supposed to be, each man doing his job, laughing and joking around, just plain enjoying each other. But the more the farm shaped up, the more trouble I faced.

Rumors began to circulate around Claysville and the neighboring village of Taylorstown that a black guy was out to cause problems. From the letters I received, the main objection to the youth home was that people feared I was going to bring black city boys into their towns who might rape their daughters, steal their cars, and bring down property values. Although most of the residents had nothing against what I was doing, they just wanted me to do it somewhere else.

People fear what they do not understand. I had feared the white man's world when I first came to the Steelers, but once I settled in and recognized the common thread of humanity that binds us all together and that this journey through life is one that we all share, I was able to see God's gift of diversity. I came to accept differences in customs and beliefs.

I understood very clearly my neighbors' concerns. Here I was, a black man moving into an area that was predominately white. I was buying up their land and was going to bring in boys, some of whom had done some pretty bad things. These people did not know me to be anything more than some ex-football player, from the South, no less, dressed in a cowboy outfit, mumbling something about getting on with God's work. Heck, had I been in their shoes, I might have been a little scared, too.

I have always been able to push, plow and finesse my way through to some mighty fine receivers and bring them down. I could pick off passes and bat away sure completions, but I could not seem to get across to the locals that I was simply trying to help kids.

The media got involved in the story and the circus began. The first articles speculated on why I had bought so much property and rumored that I might be planning to establish a youth home like the one I had in Georgia. Then articles confirming my plans were printed. Soon the newspapers were flooded with phone calls and letters from concerned citizens. Interviews with me and the townspeople began.

At first, it looked as if I had bought property that would not be zoned for the use I had intended. However, after a few meetings with Tom Wright, the chairman of the township board of supervisors, and other town officials, things began to look promising, and I started to see the light again.

I was handed a detailed list of all the people I had to meet and things I had to do before the supervisors could vote on whether to approve or reject the project. One requirement was that a town meeting be held. I wanted an opportunity to speak casually with the folks in the area, so I arranged to meet with them at an informal town meeting.

That meeting was probably one of the scariest days of my life. I had brought a good friend, Donna Lindor, with me, a well-spoken, very dignified white lady. I thought her presence and endorsement of the project would help the townspeople understand my true intent.

It was already dark when we drove up to the meeting hall. The yellow light that shone through the windows looked inviting and warm. It was a scene that Norman Rockwell might have painted.

"I have a good feeling about this," I said to Donna as I looked for a parking space. "Look how many people have turned out."

"I'm not sure if that's a good sign or not, Mel," she said, pointing to a couple of police cars.

I parked the car about a block from the hall, and we walked up the street past a small white church, a country store, and a row of homes with large front porches.

"I like front porches," I said, noticing an empty rocking chair moving slightly in the spring breeze. "It reminds me of home."

As we neared the hall, voices began to fill the air. It sounded like a thousand people all speaking at once. Suddenly, my good feeling turned sour. There was something in the tone of those voices that made me shudder.

"Are you sure you want to go in there?" Donna asked, stopping short of the steps.

I followed her gaze to the local cop standing in the middle of the doorway. His legs were slightly spread apart, his hat in place, his hand on his gun. I adjusted my Stetson and, as we squeezed by him, I half-expected him to say, "Go ahead, make my day."

The atmosphere of the gathering hung heavy with fear and anger. "I didn't think this town had so many people in it," I whispered to Donna.

"Mel, this is not going to be a walk through the park," she whispered back. "I think some of these people were brought in to cause trouble."

Silence fell upon the room as Donna and I took our seats in the front row. I was hastily introduced as the football player who was thinking about starting a youth home in Claysville. After that introduction, the objections and accusations began to fly in every direction, and a simple town meeting turned into a free-for-all.

I answered all the questions I could possibly answer about the boys who would be participating in the program, the kind of buildings I had in mind and the type of care the boys would receive. I even passed out a brochure on the youth home in Vidalia.

"Our program is successful there," I explained. "And it will be successful here."

Then, after all my talking and explaining, one woman jumped up from her chair. "That man," she said, pointing at me, "says he has such a terrific program. Well, if that's the case, why didn't he come to us at the start and tell us what he was going to do? Why did he have to sneak around? And another thing. I think the supervisors are deliberately keeping everything hush-hush. What are they trying to hide from us? We want some hard answers."

I was at a loss. I could not think of any other way to explain the youth home and my intentions. I had already answered each and every question a dozen times, and I realized that what my momma had said was true: A man convinced against his will just holds the same opinion still.

"Thank you good folks for leaving your homes this

evening and sharing your thoughts with me," I said, picking up my hat. "But I kept you here longer than I should have. Sometimes, when I get to talking about this youth home dream of mine, I just keep going on and forget to stop. You all have a good evening and God bless you."

"Guess them niggers haven't learned to stay away from our women," a young man grumbled under his breath as Donna and I walked by.

"Just keep moving," Donna whispered to me. I clenched my fists and looked straight ahead.

To my surprise, we made our way through the front door, down the steps, and onto the sidewalk without having a riot break out. We turned the corner and came face-to-face with Clint Eastwood's soul mate, only this time he was holding the gun in his hand. We stepped off the sidewalk onto the street and quietly walked to the car.

Somehow, the front porches didn't seem like home anymore.

chapter four

The Lines Are Drawn

We must learn to live together as brothers or perish together as fools.

Martin Luther King

D A Y S   T U R N E D   into weeks, and still there was no decision regarding the zoning of the farm. I had to keep reminding myself to remain patient and allow things to unfold the way the Lord saw fit, but try as I might to keep calm, I found myself growing more frustrated with each passing day.

The meetings I had with the townsfolk, the zoning board, and the supervisors did not clear up the rumors regarding the youth home. Some concerned citizens from the area banded together and hired a lawyer, who accused the zoning board of violating the township zoning ordinance and of concealing the truth about the home. Everyone was in an uproar because I had spoken with the zoning board before I had filed a formal request to change the zoning of the farm from agricultural to institutional. Of course, I hadn't known I was supposed to do that.

The official town meeting was postponed time and time again to give the supervisors a chance to address the lawyer's allegations and calm down the local citizens.

I applied for the zoning permit as I was instructed to do, but the commissioner stamped it "incomplete," saying that it lacked substance and that I would have to refile.

I am the first to admit that I am by no means a detail man. I know how to set goals, and I am willing to pursue my vision like a hound after a rabbit. However, one thing that has tripped me up on more than one occasion is all that "detail stuff" that bureaucrats find so necessary.

Someone once described me as being "panoramic" in the way I view life. They were right. I see the whole picture but miss the intricate details that go into making it. I'm grateful for this ability, for it has often been helpful to me, but it sure can lead to a messy desk, misplaced phone numbers, and tiny gaps in a puzzle. To a writer, the detail man is the editor. To the businessman, it's the accountant. To the football player, it's the coach. And to the visionary, it's the believer. At that moment, I did not have anyone believing in me but myself.

I went about supplying more information to the supervisors. Again I was delayed. This time I had to get the township's approval to subdivide the property. Then came the demand for a detailed explanation of the sizes and type of construction of the buildings, the number of residents of each cabin, and a topographical map and site plans. The list was soon expanded to include the specs of the sanitation facilities, sewage disposal, water supplies and fire protection, plus architectural drawings.

When I was not occupied with filling out forms, I was busy clearing the way for the birth of the home. I started to construct new fences around the farm, arranged tentative dates for laying the foundations of the first three cabins, and worked at carving dirt roads into the hillside that would someday lead to the boys' lodgings.

One day while I was working around the farm, I heard an unfamiliar voice calling to me from a car that was parked below on the main road.

"Mel!" shouted the man. "Looks like you're back in training. Thinking about going back to the Steelers?"

"Naw, just getting ready for my boys," I called, wiping sweat from my forehead.

"Well," said the stranger, shaking his head, "it looks like the Steelers have a better chance of winning this year's Super Bowl than you have of getting this place approved."

"Maybe so," I answered. I felt like Noah building his ark in the desert while others stood by and ridiculed him. But just as Noah knew that it would rain, I knew that this youth home would be approved.

More time passed, and summer began closing in on spring. Still no approval for the home. I was sitting at my desk, filling out yet another form and growing tired of all the paperwork. I just could not make sense of the delays. Each day that I was held up was another day that the shadow children wandered through the streets and risked being lost forever in the darkness.

I threw my pencil down on the desk and stared out the window to the weather-beaten barn. A storm was brewing. As I watched, the wind ripped a board from the barn roof with a great, splintering crack. One day, I promised that big old barn, I'll mend your holes and paint you up real pretty. Just hold on a little longer. *Maybe I'm not much different from that barn*, I thought—*worn, old and useless.*

The phone rang, jolting me from my thoughts, and I answered it.

"Hey, Mel!" The familiar voice of Andy Russell greeted me. "I got some good news for you, buddy."

"I sure could use some right about now," I replied. Whether Andy brought good news or was just calling to say hello, his cheerful, sincere voice was always a treat to hear.

"Well, pal," he said, "we're gonna hold a sports banquet for our Hall of Famers. We're gonna auction off some stuff the players have donated, charge a couple hundred a plate, whatever, and the money we raise will go to the home."

I paused for a few moments. Andy, who owed me nothing, was still giving me a lot. His friendship and support could not have come at a better time.

"Mel," Andy said jokingly, "don't tell me I finally found a way to sew up that mouth of yours?"

I chuckled, "Nope, I was just taking a minute to thank the Lord for sending me some help."

"Jim Roddey and I are co-chairmen of the banquet," Andy said, without wasting any words. "He'll call you with the details. Gotta go."

Andy's news was as refreshing as a cold glass of water to a thirsty man, and my mouth had been pretty dry for a couple of weeks. "God bless you, Andy," I said, but he had hung up before my words reached him.

Being together with my friends and teammates, even for one evening, would carry me a long way. For a moment I thought back to our glory days. We were only kids when we were first brought on by the Steelers, and a couple of us could easily have taken the wrong path. Fortunately, we were all blessed with a sense of commitment to each other as well as to the game.

A flash of white caught my eye and I noticed an envelope that had been slipped under the front door. I picked it up and saw it was addressed to "the nigger of the house."

I slowly opened it, debating whether or not I really wanted to read the contents. Finally, I pulled the letter out and unfolded it. After taking a deep breath, I stared long and hard at the leaflet I held in my hands. The headline screamed: "Negro Is Related to Apes—Not White People." There was a picture of a black woman resembling an ape, with a caption claiming she was the result of a black woman's mating with an ape. Another picture was of a black man resembling an ape, with the caption: "They can run like the wind and scale trees." Other statements claimed that the Negro skull and brain were still in the ape stage and, as recently as a few hundred years ago, Negroes had tails. Then something caught my attention. At the bottom of the flyer was an address in case I wanted to order extra copies.

Yeah, I thought, *I could get a couple of dozen of these and send them with my Christmas cards.*

What in creation stirs someone to write such things? Fear? Hatred? Maybe it is failure—failure to believe that God did not make any mistakes when He created us. God's most amazing gift is that He made us all unique, all different. A flat world that had only daisies, maple trees, robins, and cats would be a pretty mundane, boring, predictable place to live.

Lord, I thought, *sometimes your people are just like Moses, wandering lost in the desert, looking for the promised land.*

The windows began to rattle as the wind outside picked up. Suddenly I remembered I had an appointment in Pittsburgh. I threw the envelope on my desk, grabbed my car keys, and headed out the door. As I was making my way to the car, thunder and lightning filled the sky, and rain began to fall.

I noticed a piece of paper captured under the wiper of my car, whipping against the windshield. I ripped the paper in two as I struggled to free it. I got into the car, placed the two halves together, and read:

ATTENTION!!!

Citizens of the McGuffey School District, are you aware that Mel Blount (formerly of the Pittsburgh Steelers) is planning on building a "home" for NEGRO JUVENILE DELINQUENTS in your area? If he succeeds in doing this, how long do you think it will be before one of these apes rapes one of your white women or mugs one of your elderly? These ghetto monkeys will bring you and your people nothing but TROUBLE! Help stop them now before they create any problems in your area.

The White Knights of the Ku Klux Klan

We are Warriors fighting for our Great White Race, our Families and our savior Jesus Christ.

I was numb. I don't know how long I stared at the names "Ku Klux Klan" and "Jesus Christ" blasphemously together on the same page, before I covered my face with my hands.

"Dad, I'm trying," I cried out loud. "God knows I'm trying." I began to slip into despair.

Then I felt my dad beside me, so close I thought I could reach out and touch him. "Don't forget the boy," I heard him whisper.

• • •

My thoughts drifted back to the night I left the farm for college. My dad had been with me in my room, helping me pack. God had seen my family through its share of troubles, and my dad assured me that God would see us through the financial problems with the farm and would give us all the strength we needed to raise my new son, Norris. Norris's mother and I were still children ourselves when Norris came along. Even though we decided not to marry, we never once considered Norris a mistake, and neither did my momma and dad. *I* made a mistake, but God redeems our sins. We loved that helpless little baby with all of our hearts.

"We'll take care of Norris and his mother," my dad promised, gently placing the last of my clothes into my cardboard suitcase. Then a stillness fell upon the room, the kind that hushes the birds before a storm. I could feel the sudden drop of air, and the next words my dad spoke clung to me like words from the Bible.

"Don't forget your boy," he whispered, referring to Norris, my first child.

My dad was always strong and healthy, but on that evening, he appeared to be tired. The lines on his face were deeper, his eyes dim, and his smile faint.

"Are you all right?" I asked.

He nodded, then helped carry my bags to the car.

I had plenty of time to think as I drove back to Southern for my second semester. I was young, scared, and a new father. The farm was in trouble, the bank wanted money, and we needed seed for spring planting.

There was something else nagging at me, but I couldn't put my finger on it. A strange, hollow feeling kept welling up inside my chest.

When I arrived at the university, a message to call my mother was waiting for me.

"Momma, what's wrong?" I asked, knowing deep in my gut that something terrible had happened.

"My dear baby," she said softly. "Your pa had a heart attack shortly after you left and. . . ."

"Is he okay?" I interrupted.

"Your pa is with God this night," she answered. "We have cause to rejoice."

I could hardly believe what she had said. My momma was telling me to rejoice because God had just taken my dad away from me.

"I don't think my faith is as strong as yours, Momma." Me, rejoice over this? Never.

"You listen to me, Mel," my momma continued. "The decision to take your pa belongs to God. It's not for us to question such things. You will grieve for your pa proper, then go back to living life and making him proud of you. Now you get some rest before driving back home tomorrow, hear me? I don't want to be worrying about you."

"Yes, ma'am."

I hung up the phone and left immediately for home. I did not cry, nor was I feeling particularly sad. I simply did not believe that the Lord had taken my father from me.

The drive home was not much more than a blur. I remember stopping once for gas and driving into a storm as I crossed into Georgia. At dawn I arrived at the dirt road that led to our farm. I was less than a mile away when I noticed that the sky was brilliant red. As I neared my home, I saw a raging fire. My family house was engulfed in flames.

I stopped the car and ran the rest of the way, screaming, "Momma! Momma!" When I saw her standing in the yard, watching our home burn, I could no longer hold back my tears.

• • •

A crash of thunder echoed in my ears, and I found myself staring at the letter that I held in my hands. My dad was gone but his strength remained inside of me.

I had survived much worse than the KKK, the zoning boards, the lawyers—the whole lot of them.

Lord, I thought, *it looks like the battle is going to be declared an all-out war, and I suppose you have drafted me.* Then I remembered the trials of Job and quickly checked my hands for any blisters that might be forming. "Just joking, Lord," I whispered.

I began to ease my car down the muddy road to the main highway. Suddenly, I saw a young boy standing on the road in front of me. I slammed on my brakes and slid to a stop.

"You lost, son?" I said through a small crack in the window.

"You might say that," he answered.

"Get in."

I looked over at the drenched boy. Twelve, maybe thirteen years old. No coat, torn jeans, muddy, worn tennis shoes, but he seemed filled with purpose. I handed him my coat and told him to wipe himself off.

"Mr. Blount," he said, "I hear that you're startin' up a place for boys."

I nodded.

"I ain't never been in any trouble 'cept maybe missed a few days of school here and there," he said, running the arm of my coat over his long brown hair, "but I'm headed that way."

"Just how do you know that?" I asked. I was intrigued. I had never heard a young boy admit that he was going wayward before he had actually done anything wrong.

"Well, my folks don't care about what's goin' on with me, and they got plenty of problems of their own right now. I'm not much good at learning and I don't have any friends.

I'm your classic case, at least that's what the principal of my school told me."

"How can I help you?" I asked, studying his innocent face.

"Will you let me hang around here?" he asked, handing back my coat. "I'm real good at fixin' up things. My dad worked construction before he got hurt, and he taught me a lot. I could clean out the barn, patch a few holes and . . . maybe you and I could be friends."

"What's your name, son?"

"Johnny."

"Well, Johnny, I could use a friend about now," I said, holding out my hand.

We shook on it. I had my first believer.

That was a bittersweet day for me. My friends had rallied to my support, and my enemies had shown themselves.

chapter five

Harvest of Fear

To every thing there is a season, and a time to every purpose under the heavens:

Ecclesiastes 3:1–8

T H E   K K K   had made its move. Almost every day, racist propaganda was attached to the doors, cars, and mailboxes of the homes in Taylorstown, including mine. I had known for some time that racism was "alive and well" in our country, but I also knew that this flyer campaign was the work of only a few locals.

I had decided not to let this garbage faze me. Besides, I had too many other things to be concerned about. My main purpose was to raise funding to get my boys a home to live in.

But the war escalated.

The local media gave daily updates on the "racist flyer" situation, and I was giving interview after interview. The last thing I wanted to do was lend any credibility to the KKK, so I played the events down as much as possible.

But the people of Taylorstown were growing fearful. The town was now being labeled as a center for Klan activity, and the locals were embarrassed. Fear mixed with embarrassment can often bring about change in people, but

I had no idea what direction the townsfolks' feelings would take them.

While all of this was going on, I realized that I was no longer able to handle the paperwork, phone calls, and meetings that were required to establish the youth home. It was time for me to call Carol Locket.

I had met Carol about a year earlier at a local business where I was soliciting funding for the home. I'd known immediately that she was the one to help me. I told her my plans and that I wanted to hire her as the administrator of the youth home.

She laughed.

Then I asked for her phone number.

She laughed even harder.

I could not help but think that she saw me as just a dumb, ex-football player making a pass at her.

It took some convincing, but she finally gave me her number, and now was the time to dig it out of my wallet.

"Hello, may I speak to Carol Locket?" I asked, holding the phone tightly against my ear.

"Who's calling?" a man demanded.

"Mel Blount."

"Mel Blount. Really?"

I always seem to get that response.

"Yessir."

"Carol," I heard the muffled voice say, "it's Mel Blount. Yeah, really."

Carol came to the phone.

"Is this really Mel Blount?" she asked.

"You bet it is," I answered.

"Prove it!"

Gee, I really like this lady, I thought. I explained that we had met a year ago. Then I talked to her a bit about the job and asked her when she could start.

"In two weeks," she answered, then hung up the phone.

A good, no-nonsense, straight-to-the-point woman. She was perfect.

I bought the "administration building" and had it parked across from the farmhouse. As I stood looking at the used trailer, I knew that Carol was not going to like it much. Every dent and defect showed, and the poor thing was so dappled with rust that it looked like a pinto pony. But it was clean, at least on the inside. No matter. It was the best I could do at the moment.

When Carol arrived, she wasted no time getting down to business. "Is my office over there?" she asked, pointing to the farmhouse.

"Nope," I answered.

"Well," she asked looking around, "where is it?"

"There," I pointed. A look of horror spread across her face. Things got worse from that point on. After Carol had taken a survey of the office—the incomplete files, the phone calls that needed to be returned, and the general lack of organization—she turned to me and asked, "Are you sure you're ready to hire me?"

I nodded quickly. "Yes, the youth home needs you." She stood silent, gaping at me. "Carol," I said, "before you say anything, come with me. I want to show you something that is-but-isn't there."

She looked at me, thoroughly puzzled, and hesitantly agreed.

We walked together through the muddy field and up the hill behind the farmhouse. "Look there," I said, pointing to the stakes tied with orange ribbon. "That's where the boys live. We have twenty-four of them now, and when the fourth cabin is completed, we'll have room for eight more. Over there is the library, and if you look to your left, you can see our little chapel tucked between the trees. There, in the far corner next to the gym—that huge building—that's the administration building. We have nearly fifty people working in there. Amazing! I feel that it was just yesterday when I had this place all to myself. Look down there. The boys are playing football."

"The stress has finally gotten to you, hasn't it Mel?" Carol asked, shaking her head.

"Take a deep breath, Carol," I said, sniffing the air. "Chocolate chip cookies are baking. If we hurry, we can get one before the boys eat them all."

"Mel, you're nuts," Carol called, chasing after me as I ran in the direction of the orange-ribboned stakes.

"After you," I said, opening the front door of the imaginary cabin. She walked in, and I handed her a make-believe cookie.

"They're good," Carol said, taking a bite. Then she added, "I was thinking, each cabin should be different somehow. We want to give the boys a sense of being in a real home. Log cabins would be good, don't you think?"

"Yes, I believe you're right."

"Each lodge should have its own personal touch. We want this to be a home, not an institution. Maybe we can find a local woman to cook for the kids, be kind of a mother to them. And . . ."

"Thanks, Lord," I whispered.

"Did you say something, Mel?" Carol asked.

"No, go on," I said, smiling all the way down to my soul. I knew she had seen a glimpse of my vision.

We walked back to the trailer. Carol matter-of-factly removed the flyers that had been placed on her car and on the trailer. "From now on," she said, "we'll keep these in a separate file. Someday we'll read them and laugh."

• • •

The media continued to cover the story of my struggles with the KKK, the zoning board, and the concerned citizens. Then it became apparent why the Lord had sent these plagues upon me. The cruelty of a few angry people had stirred folks into action. Donations of money, time, building material, food, and clothing came pouring in. The townsfolk who had remained silent during the zoning controversy began to speak up in support of the youth home.

It was turning out to be one of the best summers of my life, for a number of reasons. The Steelers had raised a considerable amount of funding; I was inducted into the Hall of Fame; the foundations for the cabins were laid on schedule; Carol had us organized; we hired a young man to take care of public relations; the official town meeting took place; and I finally won my "conditional" zoning permit. Best of all, the first cabin was well on its way to being completed.

Sandwiched between those accomplishments, however, were occasional pockets of trouble. Early in August, another scary moment presented itself with a bang.

It happened while I was a guest of honor at the Football Hall of Fame Inductees' Dinner at the Convention Center in Canton. I was proud that by Saturday I would have reached the pinnacle of a football player's glory. Jersey number 47 would soon come to rest with full honors beside those of other Steelers that had already been placed in the Hall of Fame. Fittingly, Terry Bradshaw and I were being inducted the same day.

During the dinner I received word that there had been a shooting at the youth home. *Oh, God, please,* I prayed to myself, *don't let anybody be hurt.*

I excused myself from the dinner and called the home from a phone in the lobby. I soon found out that two local men in their early twenties had driven up to the front driveway of the property, circled the farm a couple of times, then fired two shots from a .44-caliber Magnum handgun into the hillside. Fortunately, a few weeks before, I had felt it necessary to hire a private security guard. The guard was able to give the police a description of the vehicle, and the two men were picked up about ten minutes later at a house in Taylorstown.

Then I found out that the police were unable to do anything more than issue citations for criminal trespassing and discharging a firearm (both only misdemeanors). The reason: The magistrate's offices were closed until Monday. I almost lost it. That frustration was voiced in my fifteen-minute speech at the Hall of Fame ceremonies the next morning.

After Dan Rooney, Jr., gave his fine introduction speech, it was my turn. Be it right or wrong, in front of thousands who came to Canton to witness the inductions—and into the many radio and television microphones—I made accusations instead of talking about my award. I used that happy national event to voice my frustrations and fears about the youth home.

First, I told them about the home I had established in Vidalia, Georgia. I told them about the shadow children, the youth home I was trying to start near Taylorstown, and about the previous night's shooting.

"Now I want to tell you about Buffalo Township in Washington County, Pennsylvania, where I'm going to put my second home for boys," I said. "There are supervisors in that township and community who, for whatever reasons, with their racist attitudes and narrow-mindedness, cannot see exactly what my youth home is all about. It's about reaching out and helping our young people. Racism is evil, and we shall overcome it, I promise you. The Mel Blount Youth Home is going ahead in Buffalo Township, and we will make it work."

Well, after that, I was held responsible for adding fuel to the fire. The media war between the supervisors and me had begun. "Blount's accusations stun officials," headlined every area newspaper.

But—no surprise to me—things worked out.

I just love it when the smiling face of God shows itself. It is the freshness of spring, the warmth of summer, the color of autumn, and the silence of winter, all rolled into one. The Lord placed me at the foot of a mighty big mountain, and I climbed to the first plateau without a safety line. I battled my way through fear and prejudice, and I hardly bothered God at all with my problems. Now and then, I must admit, there were times when I felt like running away. Jonah was my inspiration to stick around and finish the job that was given to me: I didn't want God sending a whale to Taylorstown to swallow me up.

But now, with a large chunk of the struggle behind me,

it was time to thank my friends and supporters and host a gathering at the home. I wanted them to see firsthand what they had made possible.

I hosted a big party to celebrate the beginning of autumn. Since the blood of a farmer still runs strong through my veins, this gathering was, for me, a harvest celebration. But instead of harvesting those sweet Vidalia onions, I was harvesting broken lives.

• • •

By late September, the barn had been cleaned and given a new roof and several coats of fresh paint. I had a couple of horses and a few head of cattle shipped up from the family farm in Georgia. This place was really beginning to smell like home. I had only to gain permission from the county and state to allow boys to enter into the program and I would be halfway up the mountain.

Our small staff had settled into their jobs and were making remarkable progress. Carol often arrived early to fill out the mounds of paperwork and frequently stayed late trying to keep us caught up on details. Mike Lancaster, our "public relations department," was doing the work of two people. He was in charge of all media coverage, setting up fundraisers and encouraging corporate sponsors. I was away from the farm a great deal of the time, doing work for the National Football League and trying to convince people to financially support our program. Our hours were long, the pay was terrible, the working area was crowded, but no one complained. We were a team.

One Wednesday afternoon, the threat of a severe storm sent everyone heading for home early, and I was left to have dinner by myself. But it was different now; although I was alone, I was not feeling lonely. As I sat at the kitchen table, munching on a turkey sandwich and sipping canned soup, I went through my mail. An unsigned, handwritten "hate" note had slipped by Carol's careful scrutiny. She usually removed anything that she felt would upset me. My first instinct was to slip the paper into the file folder marked *Carol*. Instead, I read it:

I, too, am a citizen of McGuffey School District. My children attend Blaine Buffalo District, and I don't want juvenile delinquents so close to them. And also all of us pay high taxes in this district so we can live Niger free. No we don't want any Nigers, if we wanted to know some we would move to the city and attend Washington High. Why don't Niger lovers do that. McGuffey is white and we want it to stay that way. And alot more than 28 of us stand on this position. One more thing, ask around, Claysville is all KKK! Did you ever see a Niger at Sunset Beach Pool? Think . . .

I thought about it for a couple of seconds, then decided to throw the letter where it belonged—in the trash. This person, at the very least, could have spelled "nigger" correctly.

I reached for my Bible. Every day, I open the book and place my finger on a page at random. Whatever passage my finger lands on is my message for the day. That day I unwittingly chose Psalm 121: "I lift up my eyes toward the mountains; whence shall help come to me? My help is from the Lord, who made heaven and earth" [NAB].

"The mountain," I said out loud. "Thanks, Lord, that's a good idea."

I finished up my meal and headed for the barn to saddle up Wind, a gray quarterhorse filly that gleamed like silver. I had learned to ride by the age of three. Back then, all we had was an old plow-horse named Red. He wasn't much to look at, but he had strength, grace, and loyalty that to this day remain in my memory.

My momma had passed her love of horses on to me. She used to quote Job as we hitched Red to the plow: "His majestic snorting is something to hear! He paws the earth and rejoices in his strength, and when he goes to war, he is unafraid and does not run away, though the arrows rattle against him or the flashing spear and javelin. Fiercely he paws the ground and rushes forward into battle when the trumpet blows. At the sound of the bugle, he shouts 'Aha!' He smells the battle when far away. He rejoices at the shouts of battle and the roar of the captain's commands."

Every time she spoke those words, I felt as though she wasn't just giving me God's description of the horse's courage: She was telling me how to conduct my own life.

I always regretted that my momma was unable to ride by the time we were able to afford the kind of horse she would have enjoyed riding. But now, when I go home to Georgia, she watches me riding through the fields and smiles. I enjoy those moments enough for the both of us.

As Wind and I raced up the path to the back acreage of the farm, I could smell winter in the air. The autumn leaves clung to the branches in defiance. What few birds were left had begun their early evening serenade. Intuitively, Wind turned in the direction of "my" hilltop, a place that is sacred to me. I sat upon Wind, watching the horizon turn red as the sun slipped quietly behind the western hills. One by one, the lights of Taylorstown appeared, looking for all the world like a tiny village that a toy train might pass through.

I gave thanks to the Lord and poured my heart out to Him in praise. I sang out the hymn, "Amazing Grace," because this hilltop was my church, the saddle my pew. Somewhere I read, "God respects me when I work but He loves me when I sing." "One day my boys will sing Your praise," I whispered toward the night sky. At those words, Wind flicked one ear back, shook her mane, and headed for home. It had started to rain.

The phone was ringing when I entered the house. It was Carol.

"We've got a problem," she said flatly. "I just received an anonymous phone call. The Klan is planning a *cross-burning.*"

"That's part of their job, isn't it?" I said, trying to keep things light.

"Well, this one is being held in *your* honor," Carol grumbled. "It seems that the Klan is upset that the township supervisors gave you the go-ahead. Whoever called wants me to pass on the message that you are not welcome."

"I've had that feeling for some time," I said, running a towel over my head and face. Although I was trying to keep a calm, even tone, it wasn't easy. The Ku Klux Klan has been a reoccurring nightmare in the black society and an embarrassment to both Christians and Americans. You can't sit down with the Klan, discuss your differences, and reach some workable end. The differences in people frighten them too much, and frightened people sometimes do a lot of damage. "When can we expect our guests?"

"Don't know for sure, but soon," Carol answered, managing a slight chuckle. Then her voice trembled. "What do we do?"

"I won't know until the time comes," I answered honestly. "But I do know the Lord will see us through this."

"I know He will," said Carol, sounding a bit tired. "But when is it going to stop? Not just the problems with the youth home but the hatred, the fear? I thought we are all God's children."

"We are, and He'll see us through this," I promised her. "It's all part of God's plan even though we don't understand it yet."

I spoke to Carol for a few minutes longer and convinced her to change her phone number. Then we wished each other pleasant dreams.

The morning newspapers gave the details of the planned rally. The Grand Dragon of the Invisible Empire of the Ku Klux Klan announced the rally date—November 11. I felt like Luke Skywalker going to battle with Darth Vader. I could not help but wonder what a Grand Dragon of the Invisible Empire was, exactly. After I read the article, I knew. It was a man who breathed hatred, lies, and intolerance, instead of fire.

The Grand Dragon called the protest an intelligent, non-violent means of self-expression that was not racially motivated, an exercise of the Klan's constitutional rights. He claimed that the residents of Taylorstown had contacted the

Klan and asked for its intervention. A "kleagle," or Klan recruiter, was sent to the area to organize the rally.

The Klan's goal was to show the state that the Mel Blount Youth Home was not in a community atmosphere conducive to rehabilitating children, and Klan members distributed pamphlets outlining their contention. At the same time, an article ran in the newspapers, quoting a local woman who had been ardently opposed to the youth home. She accused me and my staff of distributing the KKK literature to bring media attention to my cause.

I felt as though I'd walked into a fog bank, and I figured I needed some directions. Looking through the Bible, I read Psalm 52, which denounces evil deeds and praises the Lord's goodness. Then I released a simple but firm statement to the press: "We are here to stay."

chapter six

The Cross Burns Brightly

He that is possessed with a prejudice is possessed with a devil, and one of the worst kinds of devils, for it shuts out the truth and often leads to ruinous error.

Tryon Edwards

I T W A S November 11. The day of my final exams had arrived. If I passed the test, I would be promoted to the top of the mountain, where I could stay for a time before beginning the climb all over again at the base of the next mountain. I knew that if I passed, the mountain that awaited me would be steeper and more difficult. If I failed, I would have to repeat my first climb. Suddenly I felt as though I was back playing college football, wondering if I were good enough to make the pros.

The weather had turned cold the night before, and the day's heavy winds had blown free the last of the autumn leaves. I watched from my bedroom window as the setting sun hailed the arrival of the Klan. I could see white-robed figures gathered at the bottom of the hill, directing traffic to a neighboring farm where the rally was being held. A few were hollering something, but their words were muddled. Several Klan members on the adjoining hillside, with the casualness of a farmer planting corn, dug a hole and planted a large cross made of freshly cut tree trunks. Two men carried a portable toilet up the hill, while others set up tables displaying KKK paraphernalia for sale. A minor traffic jam occurred on the winding backroad as people stopped to witness the hooded spectacle. Uniformed police officers stood alongside the road, ready to stop any confrontation between Klan members and those that protested the Klan.

For weeks, people from the surrounding towns and cities struggled to make sense out of the Klan's actions. Most people, whether or not they agreed with the youth home, did not endorse the Klan or have any sympathy for the Klan and their beliefs.

Support came for my side in many forms: The newspapers were filled with letters to the editors saying that the rally was an embarrassment to the community. Clergymen held prayer services, and a local lumber company donated lumber to help with the building of the cabins. Boys from a local college fraternity took turns sitting in a tree to raise money for the home and draw attention to the needs of troubled youth.

Then came dissention among the troops. Fortunately, it wasn't happening within our ranks.

The efforts of the Concerned Citizens Group to mount a public campaign against the home came to an abrupt halt when people assumed the Group was linked to the KKK. The Group accused the Klan of hurting their cause (blocking further development of the home), and loudly proclaimed that the Group's actions were not racially motivated.

Then the Klan members started to bicker among themselves. The Imperial Wizard of the White Knights claimed responsibility for the flyer campaign, while the Grand Dragon of the Invisible Empire took credit for arranging the cross-burning. The White Knights accused the out-of-town Invisible Empire of stepping in and taking the spotlight after the White Knights had done all the work. The Invisible Empire responded by calling the White Knights a splinter "militant group," but invited them to attend the rally, nevertheless. To my way of thinking, they had to be

69

pretty puny people, squabbling and pecking at each other and calling themselves names like *dragons* and *knights*. Of course, dragons and knights never did get along too well.

As I stood at the window, watching the hooded figures, I began to feel cold. The voices became clearer. The words *nigger, nigger, nigger* were being sung like a "hallelujah" or "praise the Lord." The chanting made its way into my home, climbing the stairway to my room like a ghost returning for its evening haunt. I shut the door, as if mere wood could save me from this evil thing, but their songs of hatred pounded louder and louder until I opened the window and let them in.

Suddenly I was once again a helpless little boy hiding underneath the porch steps of my granddad's farmhouse. I could feel the cool, red Georgia clay as I dug my fingers into the ground, desperately trying to stop my tears. I watched from the narrow space as a mob of angry white men, with ropes dangling from one hand and torches held high in the another, searched the nearby woods. I could hear them shouting to my granddad and could see them approaching the house. "Hey, old man, where's that nigger son of yours?" Once again, I was living one of the most terrifying nightmares of my life.

Our white neighbors were demanding that my granddad hand over to them my Uncle George, whom they accused of raping a white woman. I could hear the screen door open and my granddad walking to the edge of the porch. He said nothing.

One man lifted his gun and aimed it at my granddad. "Listen, old man, we have no cause with you. All we want is that nigger son of yours, that no-good nigger that's only fit for hangin'. A no-good nigger son ain't worth no father dyin' for."

Still my granddad stood silent.

"Turn him over, old man," the man warned, as his finger played upon the trigger.

For a moment I forgot my own fear and struggled to free myself from my hiding place. I ran to my granddad's side and shouted, "Leave my grandpa be, you hear me? Go away or . . ."

"Or what?" the man interrupted me. "Maybe we should string you up along with your uncle, pick-a-ninny. Kill you before you start goin' 'round rapin' our women, too."

My granddad pushed me behind him. As I stood there peering around his legs, I watched the empty sleeve of his shirt move in the breeze. *Look at all of these able-bodied men against a one-armed old man*, I thought. *The cowards.*

Granddad took a few steps forward, almost losing his balance as he made his way down the stairs. He addressed every one of those men by name and called them "neighbor."

"John, you know my boy didn't do what you're accusin' him of," he said. "You know the truth. And you, Hank, you know the truth. Please, let's have no killin' this night."

They talked for a while. The voices rose and fell. The crickets were silent, and the air was thick with the smell of honeysuckle. I was proud to be black, and I didn't understand why these people were trying to fill me with fear and make me feel ashamed of being the color God had made me.

After a while, the mob transformed into a gathering of neighbors and the subject of conversation turned from rape to planting. A few broken pieces of laughter sounded through the darkness, then they all went away as if nothing important had happened.

I did not find out for many years later that my Uncle George was having an affair with a married white woman. When her husband found out, he called it rape.

The voices outside grew louder, and the tone was laced with frenzy. It was at that moment that I discovered that I had been carrying with me the guilt of a little boy who was angry with God for making him black.

The time to act had come. Our heritage carries with it both weaknesses and strengths. My next move would determine if I would bring honor or dishonor to my granddad.

I pulled on my cowboy boots, put on my riding coat, and carefully placed my Stetson upon my head. I knew what I had to do. I was so determined that even the wind, blowing hard and cold, would have to think twice before sweeping my hat from my head. My granddad had prepared me for this moment. I took a deep breath. I was ready.

I opened the front door and made my way steadily down the hillside as the frost-laden grass crunched under my boots. The glare of the setting sun shielded the robed Klan members from me, but I knew they saw me when I heard someone shout, "Oh, my God, there's Mel Blount! He's gotta be crazy."

Their chanting stopped. Only the howling of the wind could be heard.

"He's got a gun," I heard the Klan members murmur among themselves. I saw one man run to his car and begin searching for something. He found what he had been looking for, and he placed his hand upon the barrel of a shotgun, raising it slightly for me to see.

I stood among the gathering for a few minutes, then walked over to one of the hooded men. I asked for some literature that would tell me about their organization.

"We must all act upon what we truly believe," I said as I took a pamphlet from his trembling hands. I looked deep into his eyes. He was very young, I thought to myself, too young to feel such anger and hatred. I gave him a smile, tipped my hat, and with my back to the disappearing sun, headed up the hill for home.

The sounds of honking horns and cheers rose from the once-silent spectators. With a slight tremble in my voice I whispered, "Jesus Christ and all the angels in heaven, thanks."

It was not over, though. There was still something that I had to witness. I saddled up Wind and rode her into the darkness. Within a few minutes, I arrived at my hilltop.

Looking through my binoculars, I could see the torches, the hooded robes, the cross.

The smells of cooked hot dogs and hamburgers drifted through the air. I could see people gather around their open tailgates, tending small grills. The fall weather, the smell of food, and the excitement created an atmosphere of a party before a football game. But this was no game: This was a Ku Klux Klan cross-burning.

The ceremony began with speeches by various Klan members. Their voices echoed through the valley and up the hillside. "We've lost our white civil rights, and we want 'em back," became the battle cry. "If we have to, we'll take them back by force." The words, empty and meaningless, soon were lost in the vast darkness of the evening sky.

I decided that I had seen and heard enough. Now I knew the test question, and the answer was so simple. What's the big concern? There wasn't any. They were just small-minded people doing petty, small-minded things. I could no longer bother myself with them.

I tightened the reins and gave a gentle tug, but Wind lowered her head, swung it back up, then stood firm. "Let's go, girl," I said, tapping her flanks with my heels. "I'm getting cold." She gave a small buck and refused to move. I wasn't about to question my horse's horse sense. She knew something I didn't know. "Okay, baby. Let's wait a bit." I pulled my collar up around my neck, placed the binoculars to my eyes, and waited.

The next few speakers had nothing new to add. It was growing colder, and I was getting tired. "Well, old girl, I'm leavin'," I said, "whether you come with me or not."

Just then I heard a child's voice. Standing in the spotlight was a little boy, eight, maybe nine years old, holding onto a microphone.

"I think we should kick all the niggers out of here. We should send them back to Africa. They're stealin' our jobs, buyin' up our land, and takin' what belongs to us. When I grow up, there won't be anything left 'cause the nigger kids will have it all. Their kind don't belong here. This is our country, not theirs."

The child paused as cheers tainted the wind.

"We've gotta show 'em we mean business and kick their butts all the way back to where they came from."

It appeared that I was mistaken. The test was not so easy after all. I was listening to a small child speaking words that sickened me, words that made me question how even the grace of God could possibly save a child whose own parents were corrupting his heart. These were no longer small-minded people but dangerous people, threatening the country's future by taking advantage of the innocence of little children.

The thoughts that had been planted in this boy's mind were like weeds growing free in a garden. Soon there would be nothing left to harvest but hate. I wanted to run away from the child's words, but I could not move. The words continued to prick at my skin. Then came the thrust of the knife, long and sharp, straight into my belly as the Imperial Wizard placed his arm around the boy's neck. I felt as though I were witnessing the fall of a child into the arms of the Devil.

"Fine speech, Son," the Imperial Wizard praised the lad. "You speak the truth as though your tongue was guided by Jesus Himself. But, my son, are you willing to join us in our fight for a white America?"

Without hesitation the child answered, "Yes!" The crowd cheered louder.

As the child stood beside him, the Imperial Wizard recited the Klan prayer about how the cross signifies Christ as the light of the world.

"This is to remind you," said the Imperial Wizard, holding the torch to the cross, "that Christ is our light, our salvation. What we do here tonight, we do in His name and for His glory. May His cross burn brightly and show us the way."

The cross blazed for about ten minutes. The glow of its embers lingered much longer. When the ceremony ended, the Imperial Wizard said good evening to the Klanspeople and asked the media to leave. Then he swore in some new members. Among them were the boy and a local man whom I recognized as a neighbor.

After everyone had gone, I rode Wind down the hillside to the very spot the Klan had held its rally. As I stared at the charred cross, tears streamed down my face. The taste of salt fell upon my tongue and smoke filled my nostrils. I ran my finger across the smoldering wood. I loved the cross. It was a symbol of truth and a reminder of Christ's love for us. How sad to think it had been twisted into a symbol of hatred.

Then I looked up, and joy filled my heart. Even that misused cross of the KKK, darkened by man's fears and scarred by flames, held God's message that His will would always prevail: The right arm of the cross had never caught fire.

chapter seven

Richard

Just as the twig is bent, the tree's inclined.

Virgil

T H E G R E A T E S T sin that results from people's fighting with one another is the trouble that we make for our children. I believe that we adults should see ourselves as the champions, caretakers, and defenders of children. They have no vote, no voice, no rights to speak of; they only have us to protect them. If we fail our children by wielding a sword of ignorance and hatred, cutting down others in a feeble and pathetic attempt to raise ourselves up, we have endangered our future.

The Klan's recruiting of children is disgusting. I was soon to learn, however, that the Klan was not the only threat to children. I found that the "system" that was established to help our children was instead using them like logs to fuel a fire so that the fireplace would not lose its usefulness. I always thought that when any humanitarian organization was formed, its goal was to solve a problem. If they were doing their job correctly, they would not grow larger but smaller and smaller until they were no longer needed and no longer existed. I hope one day that the Mel Blount Youth Homes are no longer necessary. I would welcome with open arms the day that children do not need a safe place to run to because their parents have failed them.

While I was struggling with the zoning board, the Concerned Citizens Group, and the Ku Klux Klan, an eleven-year-old boy named Richard was roaming the streets of Pittsburgh in search of food and shelter. Fortunately, the county had issued us temporary and conditional licensing so that when Richard was taken off the streets, he was brought to us instead of juvenile hall.

Richard arrived shortly after Thanksgiving. He was tall for his age, mostly all arms and legs. Even though he was on the thin side, he was strong. He was our first child, and we showered upon him the joy and attention that proud parents give their newborn.

For months, Richard was the only boy staying at the home. He and Carol grew very close, I spent more time with Richard than with any other boy who has come our way since.

I'll never forget the first time that Richard walked into the barn. When he saw the cows and horses, I thought he would turn and run back to the farmhouse.

"Th–th–they're big," he said, refusing to go anywhere near the animals. "And they stink."

"Yeah, they do have a certain aroma about them," I said, reaching for a shovel and handing it to him. "There's a way to remedy most of that problem."

"What do you expect me to do with this?" he asked.

I looked down at the floor, then pointed to a pile of manure between a cow's feet.

"Oh–h–h, no!" Richard cried, shaking his head. "I'm not cleanin' up that stuff. No, sir. No way."

"Okay, I'll clean the barn today," I said, taking the shovel from him, "but tomorrow is your turn, so you better start becoming friendly with these critters. Go on over and introduce yourself."

"Like how?" he said, twisting his face as if he had just sucked on a lemon.

"Tell 'em your name."

"I don't think this is gonna work. Animals don't like me much. I got bit by a dog once and . . ."

"No more excuses. Just do it."

"I've never even been to a zoo," he said, refusing to move. "They're the biggest livin' things I've ever seen. Do they bite?"

"Come here," I said, taking him over to one of the cows. "Richard, this is Nellie. Nellie, Richard. Now pet her."

"Uh-uh!"

"Go on, scratch her ears," I said. "She's not gonna bite you."

Hesitantly, Richard placed his fingers upon Nellie's head, rubbed her for a moment, then backed away. I introduced him to the rest of the livestock, but it wasn't until Richard met Wind that he began to feel comfortable.

"Richard, this is Wind," I said, handing Richard a sugar cube. "She's my real close friend, and I want her to be your friend, too."

Richard stared at the sugar cube, then popped it into his mouth. As he crunched down on it, I felt a chuckle building up inside me. *Well, I thought, I've got to be more careful. I can't take anything for granted.*

"Wind likes sugar, too," I said, handing Richard another cube. "Why don't you give her some?"

"Yeah, sure, all right," he answered. "Hey, why not?"

I showed him how to offer sugar to a horse on the flat of his hand. He bravely held out his palm. Wind took the sugar, then nudged Richard with her head, causing him to stumble backward.

"Hey," he said, stepping back a bit. "Why did she do that?"

"It's a horse's way of saying she likes you."

"No kidding?"

"No kidding."

Conversations with Richard were not always as delightful as the one we had that day in the barn. Most of our talks were difficult and painful. When Richard talked about his life, he would only reveal little bits of information that I would have to piece together. Most of what I knew came from the police report and his caseworker, and that did not give me much to go on.

In his desperation to communicate, Richard's words would often tumble and fall like dominoes, one into the other, knocking down the thoughts he tried to express. Often he would become frustrated and embarrassed over his inability to articulate his problems and would pound his fist on his bed or the floor, searching for a way to be understood. The public school had told us that Richard had a short attention span and was learning-disabled. Later, we found out that he was dyslexic.

Snow had been falling for days, transforming the farm into a winter playground for Richard. He skated on the frozen pond, rode his sled down the hillside, and built a snowman complete with black top hat and broom. The trailer was turning into a Christmas wonderland as Richard and Carol decorated the office with red ribbons, fat Santa Clauses, and smiling reindeer.

Richard was happy and showing signs of trust. Carol's love and patience were mainly responsible for the changes in Richard. He had become a part of her family and spent most evenings and weekends at her home. He was looking forward to having a "real Christmas with a real family."

Everything seemed to be going great. Richard was progressing faster than we had expected. But the day I returned from a week-long tour with the NFL, I found that Richard had not had such a good week. Carol was deeply concerned over the boy's frequent temper tantrums, his refusal to carry out his daily tasks around the farm, and his lack of interest in Christmas, just a few days away.

"He won't talk to me," Carol said, struggling to hold back her tears. "He's angry about something, and I don't know what to do."

"I'll speak with him," I promised. The warmth Carol had in her heart for that child could easily have melted the

December snow and caused the crocuses to rise through the ice.

I found Richard hiding in the barn. "Come here, boy," I said, "I know you're in here."

There was no answer.

"Richard, I'm not going to hurt you." I kept my voice low and even. "Carol's real upset and she's very worried about you."

Still no answer, but I heard a movement in Wind's stall.

"You know, Richard, sometimes guys have problems and the only one they can tell them to is another guy. I'm here to listen, just like my dad was there to listen to me."

"Yeah, you say that now," Richard said accusingly, as he stepped from Wind's stall. "But where were you? You weren't here to help us set up the manger. You promised you would help. I'll bet you didn't even notice it!"

"I saw it," I answered him. "And it looks real good. Did you build the manger yourself?"

"No, Johnny and his dad helped. Johnny's dad is super at building things. I told him you could give him a job building the next cabin."

"I think we can work that out," I said, offering him my hand. "What do you say we go take a look at the Child and those three Wise Men?"

Richard laughed hesitantly and took my hand. "Well, okay," he said. "That is, if you really want to."

"I want to," I assured him.

We trudged through the snow to the hill where Johnny and Richard had erected a large wooden Nativity scene. As we stood looking at the manger, Richard began to tell me about his own family. It was the first and only time Richard allowed me to enter into his world so fully, and he took me to a place that nearly broke my heart.

"You know why I left home?" he began, staring down at the Christ Child. He did not wait for my answer but continued, as though lost in the past. "Because I kept gettin' in everybody's way. No one really has time for someone like me. Why should they? I can't write very good and readin'

. . . forget it. It wasn't my idea to leave, you know. But I did think about runnin' away lots of times. When things got bad between me and my mom, I used to imagine findin' my dad. He left when I was just a kid, but I still remember him. My mom said he was nothing but a drunk, but I don't remember him that way. My Aunt Irene told me he was livin' somewhere in Pittsburgh, on Liberty Avenue. A friend drove me down there once, but I couldn't find him."

Richard paused for a moment, but he did not take his eyes away from the figure of the Child.

"Everything was going pretty good for a while. I was keepin' real quiet and stayin' outta my mom's way. She was doin' all right, too. She got a job in a store, and I helped out by watchin' my baby sister. Then my mom brought her new boyfriend, Jay, home to live with us. At first he was okay. He gave me a couple dollars here and there. He even took me to a ballgame. But I knew his kind. I didn't trust him. You can always tell who's bein' nice to you 'cause they like you and who's just usin' you.

"Then one night, my mom and Jay got into this awful fight. The next thing I know, he was draggin' me outta bed and he beat the sh—, sorry, crap, out of me. Bloodied my nose real bad. The next morning, my mom shoves ten bucks into my hand and sends me packin'. She told me to get out before Jay woke up and never to come back.

"You know, Mr. Mel, I never cried. It ain't no use, anyway. I was pretty street-smart, and I never got into any trouble out there. I never stole anything or hurt anyone. I knew enough to stay away from the crazies and the police.

"If I tell you something, you'll keep it between you and me, okay?" he asked, looking up. "Don't even tell Mrs. Carol, all right?"

"It's a promise," I said, crossing my heart.

"I found my dad."

"You did?" I said, unaware that his father was still alive.

"Yep. I found him down on Liberty, livin' under a fire escape." Richard's gaze returned to the manger. "I knew him right away. He didn't recognize me at first. 'Course I've grown a lot, but I told him who I am, and he remembered me.

"I wasn't really expectin' him to take me in or anything. I just wanted to see him, that's all. So when he told me to move on, that was all right with me. 'Hey, boy,' he called after me, 'make your daddy proud. Become one of them smarty heart doctors or something.' Then he started laughin'. Why do you think he laughed, Mr. Mel?"

"I'm not sure, Richard," I said, closing my eyes. How could a father be so cruel as to ridicule his own son? In my mind's eye, I could see that little boy who had spoken at the Klan rally. He had parents. They probably did not make fun of him, but what did they teach him? Richard had no one, but his heart was pure. The world sometimes doesn't make any sense to me. Sometimes I find myself asking, "Why Lord?"

"Richard, maybe your dad was happy to think of you being so successful."

"Never thought of it that way before," he said.

Then I saw the light. Richard was angry with me. He was afraid that I was not coming back—that I, like the rest of the adults in his life, would abandon him.

"Richard," I said, turning him around to face me. "Sometimes I have to be away from the home. I'm working to raise money so other boys can live here. There will be times when I'm gone for a couple of weeks at a time. Believe me, I wish I never had to leave you and the farm, but I have to. I'll always come back, though. I'll always be here for you. Don't you ever forget that."

Richard's eyes shone bright with tears, then he turned and ran behind the manger.

I followed him and was greeted with a snowball to the side of my head. I guess the surprised look on my face was a sight to see because Richard's laughter leaped to the sky and joined the stars.

"I'll give you to the count of ten," I warned him. Richard did not waste any time making tracks in the freshly fallen snow, pelting me with snowballs as he ran. I returned fire.

"What happened to you two?" Carol asked, as we entered the trailer a few minutes later. "You look like two lost snowmen. Richard, where is your other glove?"

We looked at each other, shrugged our shoulders and laughed. It was our secret, just Richard's and mine, and we didn't want to share it.

Richard left that evening with Carol and would stay with her during the holidays. Before he left, he wished me a merry Christmas. "You're not spendin' Christmas alone, are you, Mr. Mel?"

"I'll be all right," I told him. He handed me a gift wrapped in paper decorated with snowmen. I smiled and acknowledged its meaning.

"I can't tell you what's inside," he said, "but Carol said you love them."

The farmhouse seemed bigger and quieter than usual. I sat in front of the Christmas tree, staring into the colored lights. Logs crackled in the fireplace. The air smelled green and spicy. I was feeling older—not old—just older. I remembered Christmas with my family when I was a child about Richard's age. We didn't have all the Santa Clauses and pretty wrapped presents, but we did have each other. All my brothers, sisters, uncles, aunts, and cousins would show up to share in a feast of ham, sweet potatoes, and pecan pie that my momma cooked for us. I would fidget around in my chair, anxious to dig into the food, waiting for Dad to finish his long prayer of thanksgiving and remind us kids why we were celebrating.

I was feeling pretty nostalgic and almost childlike. I thought I would treat myself to an early Christmas present and open the gift Richard had given me. Chocolate chip cookies!

As I munched on the cookies, I remembered my first Christmas with Norris. I was not much of a father then, and I hadn't improved much for his second, third, or fourth Christmas. Now Norris was just about to share his first

Christmas with his daughter. My granddaughter. Mel Blount: grandfather. I shook my head. Me, a grandfather? I really had no idea what kind of grandfather I would turn out to be, but I wanted to find out. I wanted Norris and his family close to me.

I picked up the phone and dialed Norris's number. After the first ring, I hung up. What was I going to say to him? I hadn't offered much in the way of emotional support when Norris married Denitia, and I should have. He had married a wonderful white woman. While our family was adjusting to its newest member, I could have reacted better, more strongly. When Norris played professional football with the Atlanta Falcons, I didn't do my best to help him out. If I had, maybe things would have turned out differently for him and he would not have been cut from the team.

I dialed his phone number again.

"Norris," I said, "I . . ."

"I was just thinking about you," he said, "It's good to hear your voice. Merry Christmas, Daddy."

Merry Christmas, Daddy. Just as the Star of Bethlehem had led the three Magi to the Son of God, those love-filled words led me back to my son.

chapter eight
The Ride

There is no failure except in no longer trying.
Kim Hubbard

T H E   W I N T E R   was typical of western Pennsylvania—
long, cold, and snowy. Like the ground, the progress of the
youth home was frozen. We had a list of requirements to
fulfill before additional children would be allowed into the
program. Carol and I worked feverishly so that everything
would be in place by spring.

Often I would walk around the only completed cabin,
imagining it filled with the laughter of boys, but for the
winter of 1990 the cabin remained vacant. It was awfully sad
to see a house waiting to be a home. It was sadder still to
think about the boys who needed a house to make into a
home.

Our lives were filled with papers, legalities, and
inquiries. Details, paperwork, questions, regulations—
those words would make a great opening line to the Mel
Blount Youth Home "alma mater."

Carol, as always, accomplished the impossible from her
headquarters in the trailer. At times the wind caused the
trailer to rock 'n' roll as if it were listening to James Brown.
Pencils would skitter across the table, coffee cups would

rattle, and cabinet doors would swing open, then close with a bang. Once Carol commented that, if it were not for the snow and cold, she would have thought she was in California in the middle of a "quake."

"I'm holding you to your promise, Mel," Carol often reminded me. "I want that big, new administration building and a private office."

"So do I," I would answer her. To be honest, there were a lot of times I worried I wouldn't have enough money to write her a paycheck. Money—would it always be a problem?

Norris and I spoke almost weekly. He kept me updated on my granddaughter. Every phone conversation ended the same way as I tried to convince him to move his family to the youth home.

"Listen, Norris," I often told him, afraid that I was sounding like an interfering, pushy father. "I need to hire someone to take charge of some special programs, and you would be real good at it, so . . ."

"I'll think about it, Daddy," he would promise. "Denitia and I are real happy here in Texas, though."

"I need to hire a teacher, and Denitia is a teacher," I continued. "She loves kids. You said so yourself."

"I'll think about it," he repeated slowly.

"There's this little house on the property that we could fix up. It's nothing to brag about—but a fresh coat of paint, some carpeting, and, heck, it's a home."

"Yeah, Dad, you told me about it, but . . ."

"Son, I'm sorry. It's just that I would like us to be together. You know, catch up on things, share our lives. And I sure would like to get to know my granddaughter." I was relentless.

"I'll talk to Denitia and let you know what we decide," he answered patiently.

"When?" I questioned. *I'm pushing too hard*, I thought, but I couldn't stop pressing.

"Soon. Okay, Dad?"

"Sure, Son," I said, backing off. "Take your time, no hurry."

•   •   •

Soon spring was in the air and Norris was still taking his time, "thinking about it." But I knew that I was beginning to wear him down.

The weather steadily climbed above freezing, and soon the foundations for the second and third cabins began to emerge from their blanket of snow. It was time to think about building again. Nellie, the cow, was about to give birth any day, and Richard held a constant vigil over her.

"I don't know what I'm gonna do when it happens," Richard would say nervously whenever we talked about Nellie's condition. "I figure she'll feel better just knowin' I'm with her."

That spring, Richard also took to horseback riding. He wasn't bad, for a city kid. In fact, he made me darned proud even though he refused to mount the latest addition to our barnyard family, a spirited thoroughbred that would kick her own momma. That little filly sure was feisty. I would tease Richard about his refusal to ride the horse, and he would answer, "I'm not breakin' her in, Mr. Mel. You do it. But I have a feelin' that horse will break you first!"

"Naw," I said, "that horse is a baby. You just have to know how to handle her, that's all."

"Yeah, well," he said, "let's see ya do it."

"In due time, son. In due time."

I studied that horse day after day. I watched her move, tried to outguess her, and gentled her to a saddle and bridle. Then, one warm, breezy day, I was ready to ride her.

She tossed her head back and forth and reared as I struggled to saddle her, but finally I led her out of the barn and hoisted myself onto her back. We were off. With surprising ease I rode the graceful filly across the field at a gentle lope. When we started up a hillside, she responded to the slightest touch of my heels and yielded to the commands of the reins. *All it takes is some understanding*, I thought. The horse was broken in, and a fine horse she was.

Then, midway up the hillside, she stopped.

"Go on, girl," I said, tapping her flanks with my heels.

She stood like a statue in a park. No amount of persuading from me could convince her to do otherwise. Suddenly, I was on the ride of my life. She started jumping and bucking like a rodeo bronco, and I was flying around like some green cowboy on his first ride. I held on as long as I could, but she lashed out her hind legs with such fury that she sent me flying through the air, straight over her head. I hit the ground with a thud and went head-over-heels down the hillside.

I finally reached the bottom, wet and muddy, sheepishly looking about to see if anyone had witnessed my disgrace. Satisfied that no one had seen the humiliating fall, I scrambled to my feet and marched right back up the hill. There I stood, face-to-face with the beast. This was a critical moment between a man and his horse. Silently, I turned to mount her. She slammed her head, as heavy as a sledgehammer, into my side and sent me tumbling back down the hillside.

Okay, I thought, as I lay in the mud, smelling the earth. *Calm yourself. You're smarter than she is.* I made my way back up the hill, grabbed the reins, and walked her back to the barn. After all, there was always tomorrow, or the next day, or the day after that.

I washed up, changed my clothes, and was ready to begin work. When I walked into the "administration building," I found Carol with her head buried in paperwork and Richard busy at the file cabinet.

"Mornin', everyone," I said.

"Good morning," they said, not looking at me. Then I heard what I thought was a snicker.

We sat in silence for a few minutes. Then Richard asked, "How was your ride?"

"Fine."

"Fine?" Carol questioned.

"Yeah," I answered.

After a few more minutes of silence, I was sure I heard a snicker.

"Where did you go riding?" Richard probed.

"Up the hill," I answered. I noticed Richard biting on his lower lip as Carol tried desperately to stifle a laugh. Then, between fits of uncontrollable laughter over and over again, they recounted my adventure with "the horse." *Humility*, I reminded myself. *Be humble.* I smiled, but I wasn't quite ready to laugh.

May arrived, bringing two wonderful, heart-lifting events. First, a human-rights rally was held on the steps of the Washington County Courthouse in response to the Klan's rally and continuing efforts to hinder the youth home. More than three hundred people took the day off to express their support, and it was accepted and appreciated by the whole community. We held an open house to show the townsfolk firsthand the quality of the boys' lodging and to thank those who had given their support throughout the past year. Between five and six hundred people toured the farm, and I think they were pretty impressed with the atmosphere we had created.

That day, many of the people apologized for the problems I had been having and were happy that I was proving my detractors wrong.

"This isn't about provin' anyone right or wrong," I told a young lady who had been questioning me about the program and my feelings on the Klan. "It's about giving kids a second chance, teaching them to respect themselves and others through hard work and discipline.

"The boys will wake up each morning at 5:30 and the lights will be out at 9:00 P.M. sharp. They won't have any time to find trouble because they'll be too busy working the farm, attending class, and helping each other keep their new home in order. I think that the boys should even help out in preparing the food—that is, if the cook allows it."

"I'd like to help in some way," she said, looking up at me. Several people that day offered to help, but this woman, no more than five feet tall and weighing all of a hundred pounds, made an impression on me. "I have a writing program that I think will help the boys learn a lot and build up their self-esteem in the process. I can help change their lives."

"What's your name?" I said, extending my hand.

"Annie Barnes," she answered. As she shook my hand, a slight smile crossed her face. "And yours?"

I laughed. I guess it was her way of telling me that she wasn't impressed with Mel Blount.

I took a break from greeting our guests. I had another headache, the second this week. I hadn't had a headache since college, when they were so bad that I thought they were going to kill me.

Somehow, though, these headaches were different. They gave me an uneasy feeling. Then, I heard a crow cawing from the roof of the boys' cabin. "Crows are messengers," Momma would say. "Most of the time, their news ain't very good."

The next morning my fears seemed unfounded. The press reports were startling. Everyone was singing our praises. They were impressed by the quality of our boys' lodging. They loved how the black, split-rail fence outlined the youth-home property, and they were in awe of the beautiful horses in our barn. The hit of the whole day, though, was the birth of Nellie's new calf, Richie. Richard, of course, named the calf."

May ended, June passed quickly, but it was not until the middle of July that we began getting some positive news. We received notification that the singing group, The Temptations, were going to do a show in September to benefit the youth home. The board of supervisors voted unanimously to amend our conditional-use permit and granted us permission to construct three additional buildings. We didn't have the money to build anything, but just like always, the Lord would find a way to make it happen. We announced that Norris would be joining the youth home as the director of marketing. Still no more kids. Surely by

August, I thought, the county would start sending boys to us. I felt so strongly about this that I hired five counselors.

Sure enough, the boys started to arrive. By late September our cabin was full, and what a bunch of characters they were! I had become a father to eight boys ranging in age from nine to twelve, with problems that would send any parent screaming for help. But they adjusted remarkably well to their new environment and the rigorous regimen of work, study, and exercise. We weren't without our troubles, though. An occasional fight would break out among the boys, landing the whole lot of them in trouble. They often complained about getting up too early and having to earn the right to watch the television, which was kept in a classroom.

One day, after the boys received their new, military-style haircuts, we almost had a mutiny on our hands. I thought I was instilling a sense of discipline in the boys; they thought I was stealing their identities. Twelve-year-old Kyle, who was six-foot-one and weighed a good 180 pounds, came up to me, looked me in the eye and said, "Mr. Mel, no man has the right to make another man bald without his permission." His serious tone of voice and the look of conviction on his face threw me a little off balance. After all, I was bald. Of course, I had chosen to shave my head. "Maybe you've got something there, Kyle," I said. "Let me think about it."

I looked over at the rest of the boys who had been straining to see my reaction to Kyle's comment. They weren't exactly bald, just close shaven. Maybe too close, I decided.

One day I watched Richard showing off his riding skills to the other boys. Richard was now a veteran farmhand, and I often heard him expound on the virtues of a horse, a cow, or a field of wheat to the others. One of his responsibilities was to introduce the boys to the livestock, and Richard was doing a really good job of riding around the field on a gentle mare. Then, for some reason, he dismounted and disappeared into the barn, with the other boys following at his heels. I waited a few minutes, then decided it was best to check out what was going on.

Pulling on my boots, I ran out the front door of the farmhouse in time to see Richard streak by on the new, unbroken horse. The other boys were cheering as Richard was tossed to the right, then to the left as he rode, but somehow he managed to hang on. The horse galloped up the hillside, back down and then up again, with Richard clinging to her neck. Then the horse started bucking, sending Richard flying through the air. He stood up, apparently unhurt, and mounted the horse again. In seconds, he was bucked off again. Richard mounted the horse for the third time as I sprinted up the hill.

Back on the ground and back up again. *This kid is either brave or dumb*, I thought to myself. As he hit the ground for the fourth time, I started hollering to him not to get back on the horse, but he ignored me and climbed back into the saddle. The next thing I saw was Richard riding straight and tall on the back of that wild filly.

"Mighty fine horse," called Richard as they passed by me, then disappeared into the barn.

For a couple of days, Richard walked a little funny, but he had gained a new respect from the boys and me.

• • •

Annie showed up and started her program. I visited the classroom a few times while Annie was with the boys to get some idea of what she was doing with them, but the moment I would enter, the boys would cover their work with their hands or flip their papers over so I couldn't see what they were writing. They would giggle, and Annie would just smile. I felt like an intruder.

One evening after class, I met up with Annie in the parking lot. "So how's class going, Ms. Annie?" I asked.

"Fine, fine, Mr. Mel," she answered, unlocking her car door.

"Any problems?"

"No," she answered, shaking her head. We stood in silence for a minute, then we wished each other a good evening. As she drove away, I wondered what she was up to.

When I asked the boys how they liked their new class with Ms. Annie, they all sang out, "She's great!"

"Well, what does she have you doing?" I asked.

"You know," Tony answered, "writing and stuff."

"What kind of stuff?" I asked. I heard Richard loudly clear his throat and saw him shaking his head slightly.

Tony, taking the cue from Richard, answered, "Poetry 'n stuff," and did not offer any further information.

So I asked Carol. Her answer was pretty much the same.

"Oh, she has the kids writing and things like that," Carol said, pointing to the file cabinet. "Her program outline is in there if you want to see it."

I fumbled through the folders and finally located the file.

"Looks like a good program," I said, scanning the outline.

"Yes, it is," Carol said, typing away at her keyboard. "Looks like we may get a grant from the Ronald McDonald Foundation so we can continue it."

"Who's paying for it now?"

"Annie," Carol replied. "She's paying for the guest speakers, the artists, the paper, and pencils. Everything."

"That's great."

"Yeah," Carol said, lifting her hands away from the keyboard and picking up a stack of envelopes. "Wish she would pay these bills."

"How overdue are they?" I asked, already knowing the answer.

She just looked at me. "But I have good news," Carol said, quickly changing the topic—"Annie's thinking about adopting Richard."

"Really?" I answered, wondering if this lady was too good to be true.

A lot of good things had been happening lately, but I just could not lick the money problem. I was taught that money wasn't important, but money sure was the central focus around this place. I felt a slight throbbing in my head. "Carol, I'm going for a walk."

I went to my mountaintop and stood breathing in the crisp, fresh air. The trees were once again yellow, red, and gold. A few white clouds drifted lazily through the sky. I could hear the laughter of the boys as they played in the woods behind me. They, like all children, had their secret place where they gathered to share their stories, tell tall tales, and make their plans. I was glad that my boys were meeting under a big old oak tree instead of an abandoned building in the city.

Lord, I prayed, feeling that He and I had a better connection when I stood upon that hilltop, *I'm confused. We have the boys, but we're running into some desperate problems with financing. Not that your people haven't been generous, because they have. It's just that I had no idea how much money we were going to need.* I had been borrowing from Peter to pay Paul, not because I wanted to, but because I *had* to. I didn't want money to be on my mind night and day.

After I retired from football, I made some real big mistakes financially. I started a corporation that went under, got sued, and placed the Georgia youth home in severe jeopardy. I had strayed from my Christian upbringing. However, just as Christ had punished the money changers at the temple, the Lord had me beat up pretty good. He saved me from greed and reminded me of my dad's teaching: When money becomes the be-all and end-all, you know you are headed straight into disaster.

I know the dangers of pursuing money, Lord, but I need it, bad, I prayed.

I was in a quandary. I didn't want to focus on money, I wanted to keep my attention on the boys—but to keep the boys, I needed money. I knew that the Lord had the answer for me. It was out there somewhere.

I remained still, half expecting to hear the Lord speak to

me from a nearby bush. Then a large flock of birds appeared in the sky. I felt a certain awe mixed with sadness, thinking of their leaving for the winter. I watched them fly across the sky and noticed one bird lagging behind. They reminded me of a dance troupe at rehearsal, graceful and flowing, with just one member out of step.

They had such a long distance to go, and many dangers awaited them. It amazed me how those frail little creatures endure such a long journey. Then, as if the director had called a five-minute break, the birds swooped down from the sky for a rest in the field that had just been plowed under. They pecked at the ground for a while, then suddenly took flight again in a wave of wings, disappearing into the horizon.

There was my answer, and so quickly, too. Many, many times I had heard my parents quote Matthew, 6:26: "Look at the birds of the air; they do not sow or reap or store away in their barns, and yet your heavenly Father feeds them," I recited out loud.

As I gave thanks to the Lord for His good counsel and saving grace, the screeching of a crow shattered my peaceful contemplation.

The sound of a shotgun blast ripped through my mind. Terror, as I had never known before, seized me when I heard the boys scream.

chapter nine

Winter of Discontent

Discontent is the first step in the progress of a man or nation.
Oscar Wilde

I T ' S   S T R A N G E   how a few seconds can feel like a lifetime. Never, even as a football player, did I run so fast. A million and one things crossed my mind. Maybe a Klan member had decided to make good on a promise. Or maybe, somehow, one of the boys had gotten hold of a gun. I could see the boys running into the clearing, with a counselor not far behind. I counted: five, six, seven and— eight. The boys were safe.

"What happened?" I called to the counselor. His words were drowned out by the boys' voices, shouting out all at the same time.

"One person at a time," I said, motioning to the boys with my hands to calm down. "Kyle, you first. What happened?"

"Well, I don't know, Mr. Mel," he said, breathing hard. "We were sitting around, talking, and then, BANG, someone shot a gun at us."

"Someone shot at you?" I questioned. Then the counselor, Pete, arrived, shaking his head.

"Someone nearby shot a gun and scared the boys," he

said. "Now you guys head on back to the house. I'll be right behind you."

"But, Mr. Mel," Henry protested, "I felt that bullet go right by my ear. I'm tellin' ya, as sure as I'm standing here, someone tried to kill me."

"No one tried to kill you," Pete said, then again ordered the boys back to the lodge.

"What happened?" I asked Pete as we followed the boys.

"I'm not sure," he said. "The boys were talking, and then, next thing I know, someone shoots a gun. It was real close, Mel. And I don't doubt that Henry felt a bullet passing by him. There was a fresh mark on the trunk of the oak tree. I think the bullet may have ricocheted off it. The bullet was close. Too close. Maybe it was a hunter."

"Maybe," I said, keeping an eye on the boys. But somehow that answer wasn't sitting too pretty with me. I could smell trouble brewing, and by now I trusted my instincts. "Find another place for the boys to play. Closer to the buildings."

I told the boys that it was probably some careless hunter that was shooting too close to the farm. I had a long talk about the dangers of mishandling a gun and how responsible hunters conduct themselves.

"Will you take us hunting someday?" one of the boys asked.

"Yes," I answered, still upset over the whole incident. When I thought of how close we had come to tragedy, a chill ran through me. This was going to take me a long time to shake off.

The months that followed were relatively uneventful. I was away a great deal of the time, giving speeches and making guest appearances, but I promised myself to be at the home during the holidays. I had talked to thousands of people about sports and the role of the athlete in society. "We are losing control of our youth," I would warn them. "Since our kids look up to sports figures, it is essential that we act responsibly and send out the proper messages to them. We must firmly guide them. We need to let them know that we care. We need to love them."

The speeches were the easy part; the doing was something totally different. Caring for children is very difficult. It's a juggling act between love and discipline. Somewhere there is a balance, but finding it is hard.

I did find a happy middle ground concerning the boys' haircuts, a tiny but significant triumph. Their hair was still cut short but stylishly. I gave in to a fad and allowed each boy to have one simple design cut into his hair. Kyle called their new cuts "radical."

I wished that dealing with Norris had been that easy. I was a father trying to understand his child. In the process of working out our relationship, I sometimes forgot that Norris was no longer a boy but a man with a wife and family. Every encounter with Norris led to some kind of disagreement, whether it was about the youth home, my granddaughter's upbringing, or what we would have for lunch. He was always preaching to me, quoting the Bible in an effort to prove a point. I quoted right back, and, before we knew it, we were off the subject and into interpreting the Lord's Word. No one else could make me lose focus as fast as Norris could. We were both beginning to feel as though his move to the home had been a mistake.

As Christmas drew near, our relationship improved, not so much because we understood each other better but because the season just has a habit of bringing people closer together.

"Look at the boys," Norris said, pointing to three or four of them stringing the Christmas lights across the front porch of the cabin. "They're working together. They're helping each other. You're doing a great thing here, Dad, and I'm proud of you."

"Thank you, Son," I said, laying my hand on his shoulder. "I'm proud of you, too, and the work you've done with the boys. They trust you. What do you say we grab a few of them and get the manger set up?"

"Sure. And after we're done, let's go over to my place.

Denitia just made some Christmas cookies, and ever since you promised your granddaughter a horseback ride, that's all she's been talking about."

"Any chocolate chips?" I asked.

"Naw, I don't think so," he said, shaking his head and making a face. "I don't like chocolate chips." It figures.

We put the manger together with the help of Richard, who acted as head foreman. He oversaw our every move. It did my heart good to see that Richard, who was once very awkward about expressing himself, was now giving orders so boldly. "You know, Richard," I told him, "I think it's time to think about putting you into a public school. I'm going to talk to your teacher and your counselor and hear what they have to say about it."

"That would sure be a nice Christmas present, Mr. Mel," he said, placing the Christ Child in the crib. "Ms. Denitia says I'm learning to read real good, and Ms. Annie thinks I'm turning into a fine writer. Just wait until you read my . . ."

"Be quiet!" Henry interrupted him, with a punch to the arm.

"Oh, yeah. Sorry!"

"Sorry about what?" I asked. This mysterious writing program was driving me crazy.

"Oh, nothing," they answered with the innocence of angels, reaching above their heads to hang the Star of Bethlehem.

"What's going on?" I whispered to Norris.

"My lips are sealed," he answered.

The boys grew more secretive as the day of the youth-home Christmas party neared. On the day of the celebration, I checked the chart that listed those boys who were on restriction. The boys on that list would not be allowed to attend because they had not earned the right. Not one name. *We're making progress*, I thought to myself. That was the first time the chart was blank.

The counselors drove the boys to a local hotel, where a small banquet room had been donated to us for the evening.

When I arrived, I found the boys, Annie, and Carol in the room, huddled together like an offense unit planning their next play. I walked into the room and was immediately escorted out into the hall. The door closed behind me. I tried to re-enter, only to find that I had been locked out.

"Hey, Pete," I called to the counselor as he walked down the hall. "What's going on in there?"

He ran his fingers across his lips as if he were closing a zipper.

I busied myself with some final arrangements and greeted guests as they began drifting in. Christmas was only a few days away. I had hoped we would be spending it together, but Norris, Denitia, and my granddaughter had left that morning for Texas and were not returning until after New Year's day. Most of the boys would also be leaving the home to spend the holidays with family. My own plans were still up in the air. I figured I would drive down to Georgia and surprise my momma. She wasn't expecting me until after Christmas Day. She had mentioned to me during our last phone conversation that her foot was sore. "Did you see a doctor, Momma?" I had asked her.

"Yes," she answered, then quickly changed the subject.

"Well?"

"Oh, it's something to do with my circulation not being what it used to be." Now, I know when my momma sees a doctor her foot must be a little more than sore, so I decided it was best for me to go see for myself.

•   •   •

"Mel," Carol said, interrupting my thoughts, "you can come in now."

As I walked into the room, the boys filed past me and out the door, disappearing into an adjoining banquet hall.

"Come on, Mr. Mel," Richard said, "the food's ready."

About fifty people shared in our celebration. The boys, for the most part, were well-behaved. It was sad, however, to watch how they clung to their family members, searching for a few kind words of approval but not receiving any. Two of the boys whose families had promised to be there but did not show up spent their evening making excuses.

I kept my speech short, as Carol had requested. It seemed that the disc jockey was ready to "start spinning records." After I had finished my talk, Lloyd, the smallest of the boys, stepped forward and requested my microphone.

"First, I want to thank Ms. Carol," he said, holding the microphone too close, sending a sharp squealing noise through the room.

"You're holdin' it too close," Kyle said, stepping forward and adjusting the microphone a proper distance for Lloyd's mouth. "Now go ahead," whispered Kyle, not realizing that we heard him, "and don't screw it up."

Everyone in the room began to laugh. Kyle looked around sheepishly, then said, "I mean, good luck."

"First, I want to thank Ms. Carol," Lloyd began again, "for loving us and taking care of us. And I want to thank the counselors and tell them we're sorry about some misunderstandings we've had. Next, I want to thank everybody for coming and for helping us. Now, I want to thank Mr. Mel. He believed in us when no one else did. Even though he worked us hard and shaved our heads, he did it because he loves us. We love you, too, Mr. Mel. To show you how you have changed our lives, I would like to present to you a Christmas present that came straight from our hearts. Two hundred copies of our new book, *Angels Unawares*."

All eight boys walked over and handed me a stack of small booklets.

"This one is me," Richard said, pointing to the drawing on the front cover. "I'm the only one throwing a snowball. I figured you would know what it means."

At first, I just stood still, not quite sure what was going on. "Well, aren't you going to open one of the books? We wrote everything that's there, and we drew the pictures, too," Charlie explained.

I glanced through one of the books and saw that the

boys had written poetry and short stories about their troubles and about their new life at the youth home. As I scanned the table of contents, I saw a poem called "Baldness" by Kyle. Who else?

"We will be available to sign copies of the books for our guests," Lloyd said into the microphone, "after we perform for you our 'Christmas Rap,' which was written by all of us with a little help from Ms. Annie. Okay, boys, let's do it."

The boys set themselves up in the middle of the room and formed two rows. Richard then stepped forward and began sounding out the beat as the boys joined in and began singing and dancing. They looked and sounded as good as any professional rap group I've ever seen.

The guests clapped and cheered as the boys took their bows. Then, to my surprise, the guests began to form a line so they could each receive an autographed copy of the boys' book. I thought perhaps Annie's program had gone a little beyond its intended goal of helping the boys with their self-esteem. They were, at that moment, more famous than I was.

As the evening neared its end, I noticed that Tony was missing. Pete and I searched the dining room, hallway, and men's room, but we could not find him. Eventually, Pete found Tony talking with some boy in the stairwell and brought him to me.

"Who is the one you were talking to?" I questioned.

"Just some guy," Tony answered.

"You're not supposed to be talking to any strangers," I said. "You, young man, are on restriction."

"What's the big deal?" he whined. "He was just asking me some questions about livin' at the youth home. You talk to strangers all the time about the home."

"That's different."

"Why?"

"Because I said so," I replied, narrowing my eyes. "We are not done talking about this, but for now, go back to the party."

"What did that guy want?" I asked, as I watched Tony drag his feet on his way back to the banquet room.

"Can't say," Pete answered, shaking his head. "But something strange was going on. When the guy saw me, he ran up the steps. He had a tape recorder in his hand, Mel."

chapter ten

Groundhog Day

Cruelty and fear shake hands together.

Honoré de Balzac

W A R   H A D   been declared.

Media helicopters hovered above the farm as reporters filmed the boys doing their exercises. Newscasters descended like paratroopers upon Carol and Norris. Cameras clicked, microphones switched on, and pens flew across paper. The Mel Blount Youth Home was once again in the news.

Just as the tulips were heralding the coming of spring, the reporters were heralding a year of trouble for the home.

While I was out of town, a neighbor reported to the media that firearms were being stored on the youth-home property. A story about the youth home aired on a local TV channel. While pictures of the boys jogging up the hillside— some wearing fatigues, others in sweatsuits—flashed across the television screen, a newscaster whispered into a microphone that, "Unconfirmed reports accuse Mel Blount of teaching the children to shoot rifles and storing firearms at the facility. A neighbor, who wishes to remain unidentified, says Mel Blount shot at him, almost killing him, when the neighbor confronted Blount and the boys for shooting too close to the property line. Mr. Blount is out of town and cannot be reached for comment."

I returned to the youth home to find that Norris had done an excellent job of handling the press. He had answered all of the questions he could, arranged a press conference for me, and opened the doors of the youth home to state inspectors.

"Well, Daddy," Norris said, "The inspectors want you to remove your two shotguns."

"My hunting rifles?" I asked. "Why?"

"Because you're not allowed to have them on youth-home property. The state law says that guns are not allowed on child care facilities," Norris answered. "Those are the rules."

"But they're in my home, hidden, under lock and key, not in the boys' cabins, for goodness sake," I said. Why were they making such a big deal about two hunting rifles? The boys were never allowed to handle a gun, let alone fire one. After the shooting incident last fall, I did take the boys to the back end of the property to teach them the safety aspects of hunting. I took a couple of shots at a ground-hog—not at my neighbor.

"Daddy, listen. If you feel strongly about having those guns here, you have to send a written proposal to the Department of Public Welfare. If they don't turn it down, then you have to apply for a waiver," Norris explained. "But, if I were you, I'd just get rid of them. The media is already implying that you're acting more like a commando than the founder of a youth home, and we've had phone calls from locals who are afraid that you're running a military training camp. I know you're going to get upset when I tell you this, but a few people believe that you're training black kids to go to war with the whites. And, Daddy, a few people can make a lot of noise if they want to."

"That's ridiculous!" I lashed out at Norris. "I'll bet every home in this entire county has a hunting rifle in it."

"Hey, I know that," Norris explained calmly. "But

you're running a youth home and the state says, 'No guns.'"

I called the reporters and told them that I had fired my gun in the direction of a groundhog and that I did not know about the state regulations against guns in children's facilities. "I want to cooperate with the state," I explained, "so I will be sending a proposal to them, requesting permission to apply for a waiver. If they say no, that's fine. I'll comply."

Overnight, I had became a source of amusement to the local media as reports that "Mel Blount Takes On Groundhog" circulated throughout the area.

The proposal was denied within a week, and I immediately removed the guns. When I was questioned again by the media regarding the whereabouts of the guns, I told them that I had complied with the state's orders. End of story.

At least, I thought it had ended. But things weren't that simple. The guns were back in the news when a neighbor of mine contacted the media with accusations that I had not removed the guns. "I wouldn't trust anything this guy says," he had stated. Basically, my neighbor was calling me a liar, and the media was reporting his venom as if it were fact. This was the first attack of many on my character.

In addition to calling the media, my neighbor wrote to twelve state agencies about his concern for the safety of the children and the storage of guns at the youth home. The letter resulted in more investigations and lots more paperwork for me to fill out.

"My dad," Norris said to reporters in our final statement regarding the guns, "has worked night and day to get this youth home established. He's put his time, money, and love into this place. He doesn't want it to fall apart over two old hunting rifles. So they're gone. Now, please, let's move on and allow us to get back to caring for the boys."

No such luck. School supervisors got involved in the whole affair. They wrote a letter to state officials at the Department of Public Welfare to remind them that the youth home was in close proximity to the local school. "We're not saying that there's anything wrong with owning a gun," one of the school supervisors explained, "but just in case Blount applies for a waiver of regulations, the state needs to be reminded that our children are very close to the youth-home grounds."

The shotguns were gone, and I had no intention of trying to persuade the state or anybody else to allow me to bring them back. I waited patiently for the media attention to move on to something else. When it finally did and the smoke cleared, I could see that some major damage had been done. The public's impression of the youth home and of me had begun to cool. My motives now were being questioned, my character was suspect.

Once again, fear worked its way back into the picture and the home was hurt financially. Contributions fell to an all-time low as supporters shied away from any connection with the youth home. "I'm sorry," a businessman said when I asked him for help. "If word gets out that I'm helping you, people may think that I'm involved in financing your youth-home army, and I can't let that happen. I know what you're doing out there is good, but in business, image is very important. Maybe later," he added, showing me the door, "once everything has calmed down."

I stood outside his door, not knowing whether to be angry or hurt. I could fight the Klan, the supervisors, and the Concerned Citizens, but I wasn't prepared for the rejection of a sympathetic supporter. Truth was the only weapon I had, and it was not an effective weapon in this war. When I arrived home from that disturbing meeting, a letter was waiting for me.

"Here," Carol said, handing me an opened envelope. "Should we be worried?"

Another overdue bill, I thought, opening the letter. If only it had been. The message was simple and straightforward: "We know you don't have your guns anymore! Now we're going to come after you! The KKK."

"Well," I said, gathering my thoughts. "Should it

worry us that maybe one day we'll be shot down as we sit at our desks or that one of the boys will be killed as he plays football?" I could not pretend that this death threat was not serious. My vision was worth my life, of that I had no doubt, but I could not make that decision for others.

"Carol, call a staff meeting," I said, folding the letter and putting it into the pocket of my riding coat. "Make sure that everyone is present. I have something important to discuss with them."

Later that afternoon, we all gathered in my living room to discuss what had happened.

"I received this letter from the Klan," I said, reading the contents to them. "Now, I don't know if it's really a threat from the Klan or from someone who is using the Klan's name. This letter may be serious, or it may just be somebody's idea of a practical joke. But I have to be real honest with you. You may not be safe working here. I won't blame you if you decide to leave us. This is not your battle, it's mine."

I looked into their faces and I saw the fear in their eyes. I knew that what I was going to say next would increase their fears and possibly chase them all away. "My gut feeling is that this letter is from the Klan and that we are in danger. The Klan is like a swarm of locusts that we can see and hear but can't run away from. We can however, stand up to their attack and endure it."

"I'm staying, Mel," Carol interrupted. "I've invested too many long hours, I've cried too many tears, and I love these boys too much to just walk away. I say let the Klan give us their best shot. We won't just endure, we will conquer their hatred by continuing to do what we know is right. We can't let their evil freeze our hearts with fear."

I knew that I could depend on Carol. She was strong and solid, always knowing where she stood. She inspired me.

"Those are pretty nice words, Carol," Mike Lancaster said, nodding his head slightly. "But you don't have the slightest idea whom you are dealing with. If you think that the Klan is going to stop at a cross-burning, a pamphlet campaign, and a few threatening notes, you're wrong. They are much more sophisticated than that. Who's to say that one of us sitting here isn't a Klan member? Why do you all look so surprised? You think that can't happen? Hey, the Klan extends further than you've ever imagined. You think they have to be dressed in a white robe and use a gun or rope to kill you? They're wearing business suits and can destroy you in ways that you never imagined."

"Give it a break, Mike," Carol warned. "We've enough to worry about, and we . . ."

"Hey, I'm only telling the truth. If you're going to stay here, you should know what you're all up against."

"He's right," I said. "We should know the truth. Mike, if you can enlighten us any more about the Klan and its activities, I'd like to hear about it."

"Here," he said, sliding a file folder across the table toward me. "In there, you'll find articles about Klan activities that have been going on across the United States for years."

I opened the folder, scanned the articles, then handed them to Carol.

"Where did you get these?" Carol asked, looking over at Mike. I could hear the subtle tone of suspicion in her voice.

"I've been doing my homework," he answered smugly. "It's my job to know what's going on."

"I'll read them later," Carol said, putting the papers into her briefcase.

"Make sure that everyone gets a copy of those," I said. I had a funny feeling that Mike's intention was not to inform the staff but to add to their fear.

"Before I came to work here," said Pete, "I did a little research myself on the Klan. I'm one of those people who wants to know who the enemy is and how they wage their war. I think Mike's right: The more we know about them, the better prepared we will be to withstand them. On one hand, the Klan is almost amusing. The names they give to themselves and their organization sound like words children use when they're playing a game. But this ain't no game."

Pete searched through some papers he had brought to the meeting. "Listen to this," he continued, pulling a sheet of paper from the pile. "These are the names they give each other: Klavalier—a soldier of the Klan; Kludd—their chaplain; Exalted Cyclops—the chief officer; Imperial Klepeer—a supreme delegate; Imperial Klocilium—the supreme executive committee. They even have a secretary known as a Kligrapp, and a treasurer called a Klabee. And they have a Night-Hawk, too, the keeper of what they call their Fiery Cross. The Night-Hawk carries it in all their ceremonies and Klavalkades, or Klan parades. Sounds almost too weird to be true, doesn't it?"

"It sure does," Carol snickered. "Kligrapp? Klepper? I can't believe they're for real."

"Hey, at least they sound organized," I offered jokingly. "Wouldn't it be nice, Carol, if I were that together?"

"You? Organized? Now that would be fiction," Carol said.

"But the Klan isn't fiction," said Pete. "Unfortunately, they are very organized and very dangerous. They believe that they're on a holy mission ordained by God. Here, listen to this. . . ."

"Where did you get all this information?" Carol interrupted.

"I have a copy of the Klan Creed," Pete said.

"And how did you get that?" Carol asked.

"You wouldn't believe me if I told you."

"Tell me, anyway," Carol persisted.

"When I moved into my house, I was cleaning out the attic and found it tucked between the rafters."

"Yeah, that is pretty hard to believe." Carol said.

Pete shrugged his shoulders and began to recite what at first sounded like a beautiful prayer. It quickly turned into something very ugly: "I believe in God; Ineffable; Infinite; Eternal; Creator and Sole Ruler of the universe; and in Jesus

Christ His son our Savior, who is the Divine Word made manifest in flesh and demonstrated in life . . . I believe that God created races and nations, committing to each a special destiny and service; that the United States, through its white, Protestant citizens, holds a Divine commission for the furtherance of free government, the maintenance of white supremacy, and the protection of religious freedom; that its Constitution and laws are expressive of this Divine Purpose."

"I think we've heard enough, Pete," I said, shaking my head. I couldn't stand to hear any more. These were misguided people, twisting the loving words and ideas of Christ until they were nothing more than the hollow, vicious sounds of hatred. I had to do something to stop that resounding evil. "Let's pray," I said to the staff.

Every head in the room bowed down at once.

For weeks after that meeting, everyone was on edge. Although no one resigned, we were all feeling uneasy, as if someone were watching us. There was an unspoken suspicion that a Judas was among us, but we had the boys to take care of, and they had to be the focus of our attention. We tried to conduct business as usual.

"How are we going to make up for the money that we're losing?" Norris asked. "We're slipping deeper into the red every day."

"We've been in more trouble than this before," I answered. "Don't worry about it. Things will work out."

"God's not going to be writing a check anytime soon, is He?" Norris asked, jokingly. "Payroll's due in two days."

Well, God did not write a check, but He gave me the means to pay people their checks on time. When my check arrived from the NFL, I deposited it into the youth-home account. Everyone was paid except me. I had deferred any salary that I was entitled to receive from the youth-home coffers. I did not know how much longer I would be able to continue going without pay and giving what I did earn to the youth home.

It was during that particular financial crisis that I met

TiAnda on a flight to Texas. I was going there because I hoped that I could persuade some of my contacts in Dallas either to make a donation to the home or lend us some money. I was fumbling with some paperwork when I knocked over a can of pop. TiAnda offered me some paper towels. Soon we began a conversation.

It was so easy talking with her. I immediately felt comfortable telling her about the youth home and the problems I was up against. Then the conversation turned toward religion, and it pleased me to learn that TiAnda was very committed to Christ and a Christian lifestyle. That's when I began to feel that perhaps this charming, pleasant, and attractive woman could share my vision and my life. I decided to ask her out right then and there.

TiAnda and I began dating, and very early in our relationship, I met her family. They were wonderful people whose lives centered around the church. We got on together very well.

A few months passed, and I began to realize I was hopelessly in love with TiAnda. I asked her to marry me, and when she said yes, I felt as if I had been given a second chance at happiness. We were married that May, and TiAnda settled in at the home with no problem, helping out wherever she could. Being a mother to all the boys came easily to her. My personal life had taken a huge upswing; unfortunately, the youth home was still on shaky ground.

Shortly after my wedding, I arranged to visit Kent State University to give a speech at the One Hundred Club dinner, which raises scholarship funds for Kent State students. Whenever possible, I take a few of the boys with me on trips. Six boys had earned the privilege of going to Kent State, but just as we were heading out the door, one boy pushed another. They all knew that even the slightest infraction of the rules caused traveling privileges to be taken away. The boy who did the pushing looked over at me. Realizing that I had seen what he had done, he turned, walked back into the cabin, headed for his room, and unpacked his bags.

The boys that went made quite an impression on the other guests. "Yes, sir. Yes, ma'am. Thank you. You're welcome"— the boys had learned their manners very well.

The chairman of the advisory board commented on their strong handshakes and good eye-contact. "Be proud of who you are," I always tell the boys. "The eyes are the windows to the soul and our souls belong to God. There's never shame in that."

A reporter who was covering the story saw the boys and became curious about the youth home. After interviewing the boys and me, he wrote a wonderful article about our evening at Kent State and published our mailing address in the newspaper for those who wished to make donations.

The Lord provided, and we received help from Ohio. I had to smile at the mysterious workings of the Lord. When I played for the Steelers, the word "Ohio" meant two things: Cleveland Browns and Cincinnati Bengals. Those two teams, being so close to Pittsburgh, were always our great rivals. Depending on what kind of season we all were having, the rivalry could be friendly or not so friendly. I've heard that more than a few skirmishes broke out at games between their fans and ours. But now Ohio was the next best thing to heaven.

When we returned home, the boys shared their experiences with their classmates and counselors. The newspaper article was pinned on the bulletin board, and more than once I caught the boys admiring their picture. "You're all as handsome as tomcats goin' courtin'," I would tell them. "Now get about your chores."

The *Steelers Digest*, hearing of our problems with the guns and funding, decided to run an article about the home. By that time, we had sixteen boys in the program, and some of them were getting ready to leave us. The conditions of our permit only allowed us to keep boys up until the age of fourteen. Richard was fast approaching that age.

"He's not ready to go yet," Carol argued. "The social worker can't find a foster home for him. His parents don't want him, and we need to keep him until Annie has a chance to meet with the social worker and arrange some kind of custody deal."

"Carol," I said, "I agree with you, but my hands are tied. Richard's been progressing wonderfully. We gave him some good training, and we showed him love. Now we have to give him up to the system and hope that it does its job. I wish things were different."

"Well, the social worker has not been agreeable to meeting with Annie," Carol said, staring out the window. "You know, Mel, I think that the social worker believes that Annie isn't the right color. That's why they're giving Richard to his grandmother."

"You're probably right," Mel said. "Everyone knows that social services will place a black child with a black family if they can. Forget who can best take care of the child. Color is the issue here. On the other hand, she is Richard's grandmother and. . . ."

"And she's in her eighties," Carol interrupted.

"Well, we'll just have to see what happens and pray for the best."

As Carol and I discussed Richard, I could see Pete and the boys walking down the hillside. I watched as he herded the boys into the cabin. "What time is it?" I asked Carol.

"About 1:30," she answered. "Don't tell me you're late for an appointment?"

"No, I was just wondering, because it seems a little early for Pete to be taking the boys to the cabin. Usually, they don't come back until 3:30 or so."

"Maybe they're having a late lunch. Ms. Emma has been feeling a little under the weather and breakfast has been running later than usual."

"You're probably right," I replied. Lately, the littlest thing out of the ordinary had me on edge.

A few minutes later, Pete walked into the trailer. "Mel, I have something to show you."

"What is it?" I asked. The expression on Pete's face told me we had a problem.

"Let's take the Jeep," he said, walking out the door. I followed him. "It's best you see this for yourself."

At first, I thought maybe one of the horses or cattle was injured or sick, but as we neared the woods where the boys played, I realized that the problem didn't concern the livestock. I got out of the Jeep and walked toward the woods. After a short distance, Pete led me to the boys' favorite oak tree. I stood in horror for a couple of minutes. Dangling from a rope strung around a tree limb was a dead groundhog. A sign written in blood was nailed to the tree: "GET OUT NIGGERS OR DIE."

"Did the boys see this?" I asked, straining to keep control.

"Yes, I'm afraid so," Pete answered.

"I thought we were going to keep the boys away from this place."

"Well, I figured if I stayed close to them . . . It's their favorite spot. I thought it would be all right," Pete said. His forehead wrinkled and his eyes narrowed. "Besides, what good is it to have all this land if we're afraid to use it? No one should have to be afraid, especially on their own property."

"Hey, it's not your fault," I said, seeing Pete's distress. I placed my hand on his shoulder. "We're in troubled times right now. I'm afraid it's going to get worse. I was just hoping that the boys wouldn't be hurt by this problem."

"I'm tellin' you, Mel, you're going to have to do something about this," Pete said, pounding his fist against the oak tree. "First someone shoots at the kids. Then, this," he said, pointing at the groundhog. "What kind of sick person are we dealing with? I'm so mad, I could . . ."

"I know how you're feeling," I interrupted. "I feel the same way, but we can't react. We have to remain calm."

"Remain calm?" Pete shook his head. "I can't remain calm. I know who did this. I know who shot at the boys. And I know his reasons. You know who it is, too, Mel, and don't tell me you don't. He's low-life scum. I say we march right over to his house and beat the crap out of him!"

"That very same thought has entered my mind more than once," I said, clenching my fists. "But that's not the Lord's way, so it will not be mine." I snatched my hat from my head and threw it to the ground. The Lord's way sure wasn't the easiest. All my natural instincts told me to hit something. Instead, I picked up my hat and dusted it off. Violence only begets violence. I would be of no honor to my God if I helped fuel man's anger and ignorance.

I cut down the groundhog and buried it, then I took down the sign and burned it. As I watched the flames, I prayed that the fire would purify the heart of the person who had committed this awful act. *What pathetic creatures we can be, Lord*, I said to myself. *Please don't turn your back on us.*

After a long talk with Norris, I decided that the best thing to do was—nothing. The gun issue had been out of the papers for a couple of weeks, and it was best to keep things the way they were. We notified the police but declined to make a formal complaint.

The boys were placed under tighter restriction. They seemed to sense it was for their own good and did not question why. I tried to talk to the boys about the cruelty they had witnessed, but I found this type of behavior was hard to explain. Soon, I hoped, the boys would forget what they had seen.

"I thought they didn't like us 'cause we were bad," Tony said, fumbling with his fingers. "But they don't like us 'cause we're black, ain't that right, Mr. Mel?"

"Son, there are people in this world who just like to hate," I said, shaking my head. "If there were no blacks, they would hate the Hispanics. If there were no Hispanics, they would hate the Jews. Then the Catholics. Then the Protestants. Once they were all gone, they would start hating people with blue eyes, then green, and on and on until there was no one left to hate but themselves."

"But how do we stop them from hating everybody?" Tony asked.

"Keep Christ in your heart," I answered, as raindrops

began hitting against the window pane. *Surely*, I thought, *the sun can't be far away.*

That evening, as TiAnda and I sat together in the living room of the farmhouse, I opened the Bible to the psalms of David. I searched for words that would restore my inner peace but could not find any. I laid down the book and began to pray, but even my prayer was unfocused and my thoughts were scattered. I was tired—tired of the hatred, the confusion. I just wanted it all to go away: the Klan, the Concerned Citizens, the cross-burning, the paperwork, the shooting, the groundhog, everything. Gone!

Then I remembered God's plan. If this was God's way of making the home and me the best we could be, then I was certain that God would give me the strength to see it through. I just needed to reach a plateau, a resting place to regroup and collect my thoughts. I was a little low on faith, I told the Lord. I needed a break.

I picked up the Bible once again, opened it, and placed my finger on a page. I read Psalm 55:22: "Cast your cares on the Lord and He will sustain you; He will never let the righteous fall." I felt my troubles drain from my mind.

I held out my hand, palm upward. "Here, Lord," I said out loud, "here are all my problems. Thanks for taking them. And now, I'm going to bed."

chapter eleven
Boys in Trouble

Children in the family are like flowers in a bouquet; there's always one determined to face in an opposite direction from the way the arranger desires.

Marcelene Cox

I T W A S our summer of sorrow.

In everything there is a certain amount of struggle. As an athlete I know that, but when the youth home began experiencing growing pains, I really began to suffer. Answers to problems were not always cut-and-dried, and sometimes I wasn't even aware that a question had been asked. I was quickly finding out that in addition to wearing a football helmet and a cowboy hat, I had to wear a thousand other hats as well. Often, it would be necessary for me to wear many hats at one time. I was a husband, a youth-home founder, a businessman, a counselor, a disciplinarian, a teacher, a diplomat, a fundraiser, and, of course, a father. I often thought that it was a good thing that my head was bald—if I had any hair, I wouldn't be able to fit all those hats on my head.

As the summer began, a few counselors had to be let go because of their rough treatment of the children. Then a couple of staff members quit because their hours were too long and exhausting. Our PR man, Mike, simply stopped coming to work. Money problems continued to plague us.

Somehow we continued to go forward. We managed to get the other two cabins completed and were now able to accommodate twenty-four boys. But I soon discovered that introducing a new group of boys to the boys who were already at the home was like introducing newborn twins to a spoiled, only child.

Eight new boys entered the home within a week of each other. One boy named Mickey, brought in from Philadelphia as a final attempt to help him, was having difficulty adjusting to the program. Mickey had been placed in several institutions and had managed to escape from each one within two days. He was the most street-wise child I had ever met. He didn't appear much older than his twelve years but had seen so much of the underbelly of life that it made him a very old man inside. He had lived on the streets his entire life, and it showed in the way he treated people. Mickey threatened and intimidated everyone in his path, including the counselors.

The group suffered greatly because of Mickey's aggression, and the boys split into three smaller groups in an effort to protect themselves from him. A group of boys sided with Mickey, another was in direct opposition to him, and the third tried to stand in the middle. But to Mickey, you were either with him or against him. There was no middle ground.

I suppose a pecking order is a natural structure of society, especially where Mickey came from, but at the youth home it would not be tolerated. The boys were given extra chores and more exercises to keep them occupied. It worked very well. Most of the time, they were too tuckered out to get into trouble.

But try as we might to keep things running smoothly, every once in a while one of the boys would show up at breakfast with a bloody nose or a busted lip. One day, I noticed that Roberto's left eye was slightly swollen. Roberto was the newest addition to our family and the most talkative boy in the group. He was also the smallest and the most charming, and his need for love was the most apparent.

"What happened to your eye?" I asked, buttering a piece of toast.

"Nothing, Mr. Mel," he answered.

"Does it always look like that when you wake up?"

"Like what, Mr. Mel?" he asked innocently.

"Like swollen," I answered, staring at him. As I walked toward Roberto, the chattering boys fell silent. I examined his eye. It did not appear to be anything serious, but I told the counselor to have the doctor take a look at it.

"Oh, that!" Roberto exclaimed, as if something had just jogged his memory. "I bumped my head against the door last night."

"Uh-huh," I said. I got up to leave the room, then turned to the boys. "By the way, you're all on restriction until Roberto stops running into doors."

Roberto did not have any further eye problems.

Slowly, the youth home's black eye, given to us by the gun incident, began to heal. The generosity of a few people helped us out. Whitney Houston gave a concert at the Star Lake Amphitheater in Washington County, and the youth home received a dollar for each ticket sold. In addition to the $10,000 check presented to us the evening of the concert, Giant Eagle (a local food-store chain) donated another $40,000. Annie's writing program won a grant from the Ronald McDonald Foundation, and a charity carnival was held in Washington County for the home. Also, a few of the boys were chosen as finalists in a rap contest, and Norris and Denitia gave me a new granddaughter.

Richard was released from the program that summer and was placed in the care of his grandmother. Of course, we all had our doubts about how things would work out. A teenager is a challenge to even the most clever and energetic parent.

The boys held a farewell party for him. Annie, who still had hopes of sharing custody, arrived with gifts and gold-and-black balloons for all the boys. She helped Richard with his speech and coached him as he fumbled with the words. As it turned out, Annie had two phone conversations with the grandmother. Both times, Annie's assistance was refused.

Autumn arrived, and we had a few great weeks in which nothing terrible happened. School was back in session, and several of our boys started attending the local public school. I was beginning to feel that the hard times were behind us when I received a call from my brother, Clint.

"Mel," he whispered into the phone, "something really strange is going on down here. Somebody's been asking questions about the youth home."

"So what's the problem?" I asked. "Lots of people ask questions about the youth home. Why are you whispering?"

"Because one of the boys just walked into the office. Anyway, I think this guy is a private detective or something," he explained. "He's asking questions all over town."

"What kind of questions?"

"Oh, things about the boys, the program, if there's ever been any trouble, where do we get our money to operate, things like that," Clint explained.

"It's probably just some reporter looking to do another story, that's all," I said.

"Maybe so, but the story he's after isn't going to be about wayward children's being saved. This guy's been at the county courthouse, checking out the deed to the farm and the youth home. He's trying to get the bank to release our financial statement, and he's contacted the youth services down here, making some nasty accusations about both homes. And that's not all. Twice, this guy was spotted talking to the boys and taping their conversations. You have any idea what this is all about?"

I thought for a moment. "We haven't had anything like that happening here, but we sure have been having our share of problems. Wait a minute! At last year's Christmas party, Pete saw a guy talking to one of the boys. He had a tape recorder, too."

"Well, I think we're in for some trouble. I don't know what this guy is looking for, but I have the feeling he's out to get you."

"I don't think it's anything we can't handle," I said, offering him what comfort I could. In my gut, I knew we were going to have some real challenges ahead of us. "But if you get the opportunity to talk to this guy, have him call me."

Before I hung up, I asked about Momma. She was still having trouble with her foot, but it wasn't stopping her from visiting with the boys, going to church, and cooking up a storm in the kitchen. Clint said she was doing the same old things, only slower. I wanted my momma to visit the youth home in Pittsburgh, to see all that we had accomplished here, but she refused to fly, and the drive would have been too much for her.

As I was thinking about Momma, sitting in her rocking chair on the front porch, reading her Bible, I smiled. I promised myself that I would call her and tell her that I loved her. My dad had taught me to be strong, determined. He gave me a focus and helped instill my vision of the youth home. My momma gave me the quiet stillness of the Lord's words. "In here," she would say, holding the Bible in her hand, "is where you find the answers to all of your questions. In here is life." In many ways, she was and still is my wisest teacher and my strongest source of faith.

"Mel!" Carol's voice interrupted my thoughts. "Mel, we've got a serious problem."

I turned and looked at her. All of our problems these days were serious, but the expression on Carol's face was caught somewhere between fear and sorrow.

"What is it now?" I asked, not really wishing to know.

"Kevin stole a car."

I heard her words, but they didn't make any sense. Initially, we had had some problems with Kevin. He had run away from the youth home a week or so after he was placed into the program, although we found him a couple of hours later, hiding nearby. For months after that, the boy's behavior was exemplary.

"I thought Kevin was in school today," I said, rubbing my chin with my fingers.

"Yeah, he was, but he must have decided that he needed to get away, because he stole the school board president's car." Carol shook her head in disbelief. "Of all the stupid things to do! When they catch him, he won't be allowed to return here. They'll put him in lock-up for sure."

"What made him pull such a knuckle-headed stunt?" I asked. "The boy was just beginning to get his life together."

"I don't know," Carol answered as she grabbed her coat. "We better go down to the school."

We found out from Kevin's teacher that Kevin had failed a math test and was told to take it to the youth-home counselors for their signatures. "We wanted to make sure you were aware that Kevin was not doing well in class," Kevin's teacher explained. "It's standard procedure for us to get the parents' or guardians' signatures when a child fails a test. If the parent is not able or isn't interested in helping the child improve, our next step is to ask the parents to come in for a meeting with us. I'm not sure if you are aware of it, Mr. Blount, but Kevin has been warned three times about his studying habits."

"Well, ma'am, all the boys have study time. I guess some need more time than others. I'll see to it personally that if this problem comes up again, I'll get it handled in short order. I'm glad to see you doing such a fine job watching out for our boys."

"I feel bad for the kid," one of the men in the room offered. "I wish we could have done more. I hope they find him soon."

"Thank you," I said, placing my Stetson on my head. As Carol and I walked to the car, I realized that the gentleman who was so concerned about the boy was the man whose car Kevin had stolen.

Four hours after Kevin had run away, I received a phone call from him. "Mr. Mel, I'm sorry," he said, sobbing. "I want to come back to the home. Please come and get me."

"Okay," I answered him. "Tell me where you're at, and I'll come and pick you up and bring you back."

"You won't call the police, will you, Mr. Mel?"

"I'm going to have to call the police, Kevin," I said, wishing that there were some other way to handle this mess. "You did something very serious. Look, let me pick you up, bring you back to the home, and then we'll go talk to the police together, all right?"

"But they'll take me to jail," he wailed. "You can't call the police."

"Kevin, I'm going to do my best to convince them to allow you to stay with us, but there's no guarantee. The police will have to be notified. They're out looking for you now, so it's going to be better for you to turn yourself in."

"I guess so. I mean, if that's the only way. . . ."

"It's the *right* way," I interrupted.

"I'm in East Liberty, on the corner of Centre and Morewood. Mr. Mel, tell them I'm sorry, and I'll be good from now on, I promise," he said. His voice was beginning to sound a little calmer. "And, Mr. Mel, I failed my math test, and I'm sorry about that, too."

"We'll talk about that later," I said, knowing that all the apologies in the world wouldn't make much difference. The youth home was not allowed to accept boys who had committed a criminal offense, and grand larceny was almost as criminal as an offense could get. "I'll be there in about forty-five minutes. You stay put and keep out of trouble."

"I won't cause anyone any more trouble, I promise, Mr. Mel."

That was the last time I spoke with Kevin. When I arrived at the corner he'd mentioned, he was nowhere to be seen. I waited for about an hour, then got back into my car. I sat for a while and stared out the window, gazing at the faces of the people passing by. Evening was beginning to darken into night when I finally picked up the car phone and dialed the police.

When I arrived back at the home, a message was waiting for me that the car had been recovered. There was damage to the door lock, the dashboard, the steering column, the windshield, and the upholstery. Charges were going to be filed against Kevin as soon as they apprehended him.

Unfortunately, the news reports of the auto theft by a youth-home resident did not help improve our already suffering image. I assured the reporters, the police, and the school that we would not violate our restrictions by allowing Kevin to return to the youth home. "Our program was not designed to handle Kevin's type of problems," I told them. "We feel he would be better off in another facility." I hated saying those words.

The next day, the police alerted the neighbors around the area to keep their car doors locked.

Kevin was never found.

chapter twelve

The Conversation

It is a wise son that knows his father.

Homer

It is a wise father that knows his child.

Shakespeare

"D A D," Norris said, barging into the kitchen of the farmhouse. "We need to talk."

"I was just about to have lunch," I said, crumbling a few crackers into my soup. "Care for some?"

"No," Norris answered, leaning against the sink with his arms crossed. "I said I want to talk. And I want you to listen."

"Come on, Norris, can't this wait until later?" I asked, lifting a spoonful of tomato soup to my mouth. Before the spoon touched my lips, Norris grabbed the bowl of soup. His actions caught me off guard, and I sat staring, open-mouthed, holding the spoon a few inches away from my lips.

"You can eat later," he said, tossing the bowl into the sink. I heard the bowl crack. "Never mind the bowl, I'll buy you a new one. That is, if there's enough money around here to pay me. I just took a look at the checkbook. It's a mess. When's the last time you balanced it?"

"I don't think that's any of your business," I answered, throwing the spoon into the sink. "I've always paid you, so what's your problem?"

"Yeah, you pay me. Always a couple weeks late, and now I know why. I don't think your priority around here is to pay people," he said, still standing with his arms crossed. "In fact, I'm not quite sure what your priorities really are."

"You of all people should know that it's the boys," I said, not liking where this conversation was leading.

"Well, if what you say is true," he said, taking a few steps toward me, "I suggest you start paying some attention to the details of operating this place. Carol and I can't handle everything. I just found a stack of paperwork that hasn't been done. If the state ever requests this information, you're going to be in some deep trouble. They could shut off funding to this place if you don't learn to dot your *i*'s and cross your *t*'s. You may not have a vision left to follow. You're preaching to the boys things you don't even do yourself."

"Norris," I said, pushing my chair away from the table. "I've gotten the home this far without your help. I'll get it the rest of the way—alone—if I have to."

The expression on Norris's face told me that he didn't much care if I had to go it alone.

"Listen, Norris," I said, softening the tone of my voice. "There are a lot of things you don't understand about keeping this place running. There's so much to do that I just run out of time. It just so happens that the day only has twenty-four hours and I need forty to get everything done. Early on, I had to set my priorities, and I did. My top priority is to spend time with the boys. The second is to raise money for the home, and that means I have to do more traveling and attend more banquets than I want to. It's not all fun and games on the road, believe me. It's work. Hard work. Besides all of that, Son, I have a job with the NFL. I can't give that up, because it's the only thing that feeds

TiAnda and me. And, to top it all off, for everything I put into this place, I don't even collect a paycheck." Norris's expression didn't change. "Why am I even explaining all of this to you? You're not in the mind to listen."

"I'm listening," growled Norris. "but I'm not hearing the explanations I need. The checkbook, the understaffing, your problems with the state's rules—you're gonna have to answer for this mess you've created. And saying you don't have the time to handle everything just won't cut it." Norris headed for the door. Without turning around, he added, "You're a good talker, Dad. But if you want to keep this home, you better get with the program. Carol and I are busting our butts, and we need your help."

"You hold on a minute," I said, rising to my feet. "You get back here and apologize. You can't be coming into my house and accusing me of not doing my job. I'm doing God's work and you don't hear any complaints from Him, do you?"

"Get off this 'God's work' stuff, will ya?" Norris said, turning around. Now we were standing face-to-face, anger to anger. Father to son. "Give Him time and He'll start complaining, too, just as soon as He takes a good look at what you haven't done. And you haven't given to Caesar what is Caesar's."

I had known when Norris came to live here that we would eventually be in this position. All fathers and sons confront each other in this way, at least once. Even though I expected this, my heart was pounding, my face felt hot, and I stood before my son with my fists clenched.

"God is this program. All I care about is giving God His due, first. Caesar is just going to have to learn to be patient," I said, not even attempting to hide my anger. "You are too young and inexperienced to understand that you can't do everything to everyone's satisfaction. And you know something else? You don't have to. One day when you grow up, you'll understand what I'm talking about."

"I know the difference between right and wrong and that's all that matters to me," Norris answered. His nostrils

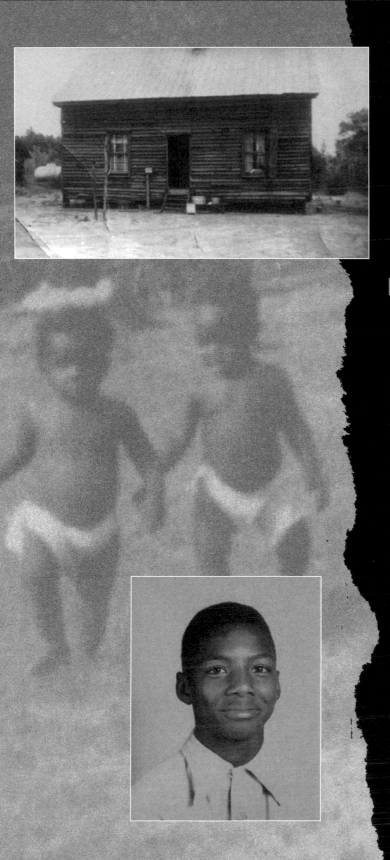

The most influential factor in my life is my family. Here is my mom, Mrs. Alice Blount, who along with my dad had the challenging task of bringing up eleven children (opposite page).
The youngest of all the children, I was born in this house in Vidalia, Georgia (top photo, this page).
This is my grandfather's log barn in Georgia, where he lived during the early 1900s (lower left).
Here I am in the ninth grade, all set for the "big leagues" of high school (lower right).
This is my older brother John, now deceased, playing ball behind our house (background, opposite page).
My niece and nephew playing on Mom and Dad's farm in Georgia (background, this page).

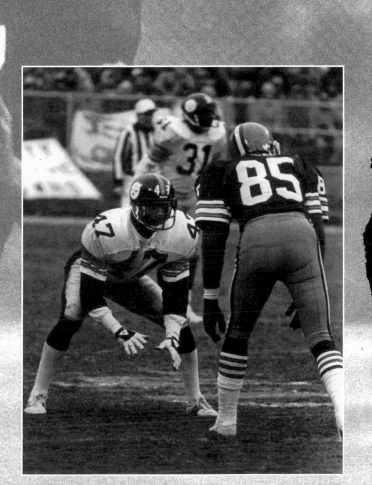

Here I am in my stance, poised and ready for action (bottom, this page). This is me, #47, heading for a touchdown (background).

One of my favorite pastimes when I am not juggling my busy schedule is cattle ranching. I am accepting first place in a NCHA cutting competition (top, this page).
I am being interviewed about the Three Rivers Stadium in Pittsburgh (bottom, this page). Team spirit ignited us on and off the field. Steelers teammates and I at the Berlin Wall, on an NFL tour of Germany (background, this page).
On the day of my induction into the Pro Football Hall of Fame (bottom, opposite page).

Seven members of the youth home and I, sitting at the home's entrance in Claysville, Pennsylvania (opposite page). The Ku Klux Klan fought hard to prevent the youth home from opening, and lost (this page).

It's important to teach
responsibility to the boys
at the home. This young
resident takes pride in
caring for the horses (top,
opposite page).
Everyone at the home has
his own chores, from
sweeping the barn (lower
left, opposite page) to
doing the dishes (lower
right, opposite page).
The boys play football and
ride horses, but the youth
home is also a place for
learning. The educational
staff helps two children on
the computer (top,
this page).
My love for kids makes me
want to spend as much
time as possible with
them. Here I am playing
checkers with the kids
(bottom, this page).
I want the boys at the
home to learn discipline.
This determined youngster
holds on tightly as he runs
with the football
(background).

In 1991, George Bush named me his 524th Daily Point of Light. I'm pictured at the White House with the President and Mrs. Bush (top, opposite page).
At the induction ceremony into the Sports Hall of Fame in 1989 (bottom, opposite page).
My own beautiful family: my wife TiAnda, and our daughter, Tanisia (bottom, this page)
My mother and I at the ground-breaking ceremony for the youth home in Claysville (background).

Children will always hold a special place in my heart. Natausha, my granddaughter, gives a kiss to her big granddad (top, opposite page).
The boys from the youth home were just as excited as I was to meet Governor and Mrs. Bob Casey of Pittsburgh (top, this page).
The first cabin at the youth home in 1990, fully equipped with all we needed to survive (bottom, opposite page).
My friends from the NFL will never be forgotten. Pictured here at an alumni banquet are (l. to r.) Lawrence Taylor and Deron Cherry (bottom, this page).

flared and he walked past me, hitting into me with his shoulder. "I know that if the state wants you to fill out a questionnaire, you fill out the questionnaire. They don't understand it when you tell them that you're too busy doing God's work. Frankly, they don't care. These people aren't answering to God at the end of the workday. They're answering to the guy ahead of them.

"If you don't start complying with their needs, you're going to be in for a rough ride. When that happens, I don't want any part of it."

"That's right, Norris," I said, following him into the living room. "Run when it gets tough. That seems like something you're good at." Oh, I wish I hadn't said that.

Norris turned and stared at me. He didn't say a word. I had dealt a low blow and I knew it. "I'm sorry," I said, feeling like a poor excuse for a parent. Why did understanding my own son have to be so difficult?

"You want to know something?" Norris asked, picking up the football that was lying on the floor. "I think you know I'm right. I think that the great Mel Blount, football player and philanthropist, doesn't know how to see details. You have a problem with me because I can see them. I'm finally better than you are at something."

"Then do it! See the details for me!" I said, raising my hands and sweeping them through the air.

"I have a better idea," he said, throwing the football a little too hard, causing me to drop it. I watched as it rolled underneath the coffee table. "Why don't you take the time to learn to see some of the details? Then you'll save us all time and trouble."

"That's why you and Carol are here," I said. "That's your job, not mine."

"Everything around here is your job," Norris answered. He bent down and reached for the football. "When push comes to shove, you're responsible for everything that goes on around here. It's you that's going to be held accountable, not me or Carol or the counselors. Just you."

"I accept that," I said, getting ready for another throw of the football.

"You don't get it, do you?" Norris asked, tossing the football up in the air and catching it. "You just don't get it."

"Okay. I give in. What don't I get?" I asked.

"You're a target. You're standing wide open, wearing a sign that says, 'Here I am. Shoot me." He flung the football at me again. This time I caught it.

Things were beginning to come together. My son's anger had something to do with fear: fear of his father getting hurt.

"You think the Klan is going to stop? Well, I got news for you, they're only going to change direction. And you've upset enough people at Child Youth Services to make sure they're going to get back at you one way or another. You think that just because you've met some of their demands that they've stopped watching you? They haven't. They're watching you like hawks, waiting for you to slip up. And when you do, they'll be in for the kill. They don't want this program to work. They want *their* program to work. You're a bad apple, a fly in the soup, call it whatever you want. And guess what? You're playing right into their hands."

"Norris," I said, holding the football. "I have everything under control."

"No, you don't, Dad." Norris shook his head, then sat down. "You don't have a handle on the staff. You hire people because you 'feel good' about them. You can't do that. You have to investigate them the way the state says you should, then fill out the forms and file them properly. You have to document their training process, give them their certificate or whatever it is that the state wants you to do."

"All right," I conceded. "I'll do that from now on."

"I hope it's not too late," Norris said, rubbing his forehead. "I just discovered that Mike stole some of our files. He could try to use the information in those files against us. He also took our list of contributors. Seems he's starting a youth home of his own over in the next county.

And that counselor that we had to fire? Well, she was trouble from the start. She'll turn on you as sure as night turns to day."

"All right, already," I said. "I've made some serious mistakes, but none we can't recover from."

"Dad, it's hard enough running this place. We shouldn't have to be recovering because of mistakes that should never have been made in the first place."

"Norris, this whole conversation isn't really about the youth home, is it?" I asked, taking a seat across from him. "It's about me as a parent. You think I've failed you. That's the mistake you're really talking about, isn't it?"

"See? You don't listen," Norris said, turning his head. "I'm trying to tell you about problems around here, and you're trying to change this into something personal."

"Yeah, you're right," I said. Gently I took hold of his chin and turned his face toward mine. "I promise I'll think about everything you've said to me. But maybe you and I should talk about us. Man to man."

"Man to man? Are you for real?" Norris said, shrugging his shoulders and pulling away. "We have a hard enough time talking about this place. We won't make it through a conversation about our relationship. Besides, you've made it very clear that I'm not a man. Every time I try to talk to you, you say I'm too young to understand. You obviously haven't taken the time to look around. I'm a father, a husband, and darn good at my job here. You think it's easy picking up after you? You think it's easy being Mel Blount's son?"

"I guess it's not easy to be my son if you're trying to be like me," I said, touching him on the shoulder. "Are you trying to be like me?"

"No," Norris said, brushing my hand away. "I don't want to be like you. I want to be like Norris. I want you to see Norris."

"I see you," I said, looking at his face. "I see a fine father, husband, worker. I honestly do."

"That's what I mean," Norris huffed. He stood up and

131

walked across the room. "I don't want to hear a list of the things I do. I want you to see me, Norris—who I am, what I'm about, how I feel. I'm not a stupid child, you know. Remember, I had to grow up knowing my father wouldn't be there when I needed him. I had to learn to trust myself. Sometimes I think you're trying to be the father I needed then, because you're not being the father I need now. Why can't you see me?"

I was growing upset. Confused. *Dad*, I thought, *did I do that very thing you asked me not to do?* Could it be that I forgot the boy? How was I going to make it up to him? How was I going to show him how much I really did love him? Had I failed my son?

"Norris, what do you want me to do?" I asked, walking toward his broad, strong back. "Admit that I've been a terrible father? All right then, I admit it."

"What I want is for you to get this youth home in order before your enemies come after you again. I want a father who takes his vision and makes it come true because he lives what he teaches. Dad, I really don't blame you for anything. If you're feeling guilty, you've got to deal with it. I've already come to grips with the fact that my father is different from most fathers. Different from most people. And I've learned one more thing. I can't stay here. This is your show. I have to go find mine."

Norris turned. And there we were, once again, standing face-to-face. Man to man. Anger still radiated from Norris.

"I've got to go," Norris said, walking away. Norris was like a volcano on the verge of erupting. I had made mistakes with Norris, and he was the one suffering for them. Maybe I would never know the full force of his anger, but I did know one thing for certain: Norris would never repeat the mistakes of his father. He was much too aware of the consequences.

I felt ashamed as I watched Norris walk out the door. He closed it hard behind him. The sound intensified the aching of my heart.

"Pa," I whispered, pointing toward the heavens. "You were a good father. I hope I told you that while I had the chance. But if I didn't, I'm telling you now. And, Pa, I never really forgot my boy. I love him."

Why was I telling my dad that? It was Norris who should hear those words. I ran to catch up with him.

"Norris! Norris!" I called, running down the sidewalk. "I have something I want to say to you." Norris slowed down, but didn't stop.

"What is it?" he asked, as I caught up to him.

"Well . . . I . . ."

"Yes?"

"I love you," I said.

Norris paused, his face caught between sadness and anger. "I believe you." He turned away from me and gazed out at the empty meadow. "Dad, I'm sorry, I really have to go now. It's almost one o'clock, and I promised Denitia I'd watch the girls this afternoon. She needs some time to be alone."

"If you need any help," I offered, "give me a call."

"I'll be okay," Norris said, walking away. "Thanks, anyway."

I could sense he needed time away from me, some distance between us. Maybe Norris had to step away from me so one day we could come back together. *Next time, it will be on more equal terms*, I thought. That should be interesting and challenging. Fathers and sons. Such a complex relationship. I had so much yet to learn, but I knew I had one heck of a son to teach me.

I was glad that Norris was turning into his own man, capable and determined, but as much as I welcomed the man, I missed knowing the boy. Suddenly, I found myself wishing that my own dad had been alive to see me grow into manhood.

chapter thirteen
Night Terror

It is so stupid of modern civilization to have given up believing in the devil when he is the only explanation of it.

Ronald Knox

M O S T   N I G H T S   sleep comes easy to me. I pray, I close my eyes, and I dream. But not that night. I had lost one child to the darkness of the streets. That sense of loss was something I would never get used to. I had lost another child to manhood. Even though it's supposed to be that way, it was my child who was gone forever, and that made me feel pretty sad.

I lay awake, listening to the howling wind. The light of the full moon cast eerie, dancing shadows on my bedroom walls. "Where are you, Kevin?" I whispered into the darkness. A sense of foreboding filled me as the shadows grew larger and more frenzied, like demons dancing at midnight.

I turned and tossed but could not find any comfort. TiAnda stirred slightly. My thoughts were disturbing her sleep. I quietly got out of bed, reached for my clothes and got dressed in the bathroom. Some nights just weren't meant for sleeping. I needed to clear my head. A long walk in the fresh night air would surely cure my blues.

I opened the front door and walked into the darkness. The force of the wind was exhilarating. It was uncommonly warm for this time of year. The moon had disappeared behind the clouds, taking the shadows with it. *Funny,* I thought, *how shadows can't exist without light.* My senses were acute, but my mind felt as if it were on overload. So much had been happening. Kevin, Richard, Norris, the mysterious reporter—all swirled around in my mind. I had had nights like this before, and I knew that it was going to be a long while before morning.

As I approached the barn, I heard the horses neighing and snorting. When I entered, if I had not known better, I would have thought that a legion of strangers were in the stalls with them. The horses were stamping their hooves, kicking against the stalls, and pawing at their bedding. I stroked them and talked to them, but nothing I did calmed them down. Perhaps there was something in the wind calling to them and to me, robbing us of our dreams.

I resumed my night tour and eventually ended up sitting on the front porch steps of Cabin One. It was getting close to two in the morning, and I still wasn't sleepy.

Suddenly I heard a scream, then another and another. The lights in the cabin turned on, and I pounded on the door to be let in. Finally, one of the counselors, realizing that it was me, opened the door and I burst into the cabin.

"What's going on here?" I demanded as the screams turned into loud sobs.

"It's okay, Mel," Pete said, standing in the doorway of one of the bedrooms. "Jack had a nightmare, and his screaming touched off some of the boys. We're working at getting them calmed down, but it's going to take a while. We're having a really bad night tonight. It's been crazy around here all evening."

"Mr. Pete!" Alton stood in the hallway, tears in his eyes. "Come here!"

I made a move to follow Pete to the adjacent bedroom where Alton slept, but he motioned for me to stay. "Alton probably wet the bed again, and he'll be mighty embarrassed if you see that," Pete explained. "I'll take care of him."

I paced back and forth for a couple of seconds, then walked into Jack's room. I was shocked to find him rocking back and forth on the edge of his bed with his arms wrapped tightly around his waist. His sobbing was almost too painful for me to bear.

I sat down beside him, but he didn't seem to notice me. He kept rocking and staring wide-eyed at something that only he was able to see. I put my arms around him and pulled him gently toward me, resting his head on my chest. I was at a loss. I wanted to say something to help ease his fear, but I was not armed with the right words to slay his monsters, and this child had real monsters chasing him, devils that possessed his dreams, turning nightmares into night terrors. *Lord, what is happening here?* I thought. What torments have befallen your children?

I held Jack until he fell asleep, then laid him in his bed and covered him with a blanket. I studied his tear-stained cheeks, his clenched jaw, his shut-tight eyes. Sleep had not taken the pain and fear from his face. Sleep should be sweet, not terrifying. *Dear angels, watch over him.* I could protect him from cold and hunger but little else, it seemed.

"Mr. Mel." I heard a soft voice beside me.

"Tony, what are you doing out of bed?" I whispered.

"I couldn't sleep," he answered, rubbing his eyes. "I think someone's in the closet."

Another bad dream, I thought. I opened the door to calm his fears and almost jumped out of my boots. Sure enough, there was someone in the closet. "Henry! Come here, Son," I said, reaching for him. "My Lord, child, what are you doing in there?"

"No! Get out of here!" Henry screamed, kicking at me as he backed farther into the closet amidst a rackful of clothing. "Don't you touch me! Go away!"

"Henry, Henry," I said, softly. "It's me, Mr. Mel. No one's going to hurt you. I won't let anyone hurt you, I promise. Now come to me, Son."

He stared at me as if trying to figure out who I was. I pushed the clothes aside and bent down. "See, Henry, it's me. Mr. Mel."

"Mr. Mel? Are you sure? Oh, it is you, Mr. Mel," he said, with a sigh of relief. "I thought you were my old man comin' to get me. I heard my brother screaming, so I ran and hid. My old man hardly ever looks in the closet."

"You're safe, child," I continued to assure him. I reached out my hand and he took it. It was such a tiny hand. Poor Henry. His father had been dead for two years, but he still raged in his son's nightmares. "Your brother wasn't screaming, Henry. You're here at the youth home. You're safe."

"Yeah, I know," he answered, rather sheepishly, as if he were almost embarrassed for having to hide to protect himself. "Sometimes I just plain forget."

"I see you found Henry," Pete said, entering the room. "Come on, guys, let's get back to bed. Tomorrow's gonna be here soon enough, and we've got a busy day ahead of us."

I helped Pete with the boys and stayed with them until they were all asleep, then I went outside. I sat down on the steps, going over in my mind what I had just witnessed, when Pete touched my shoulder.

"Hey, Mel," he said, sitting down beside me. "What do you say we get a porch swing for out here? It would be a darn sight more comfortable than these steps."

"Yep, you're right," I said, nodding my head. "You know, I think a rocking chair might be a good idea, too. Where I grew up, every porch had a rocking chair, and no matter what the time of day, someone was always in it. Kind of made me feel safe. There was always someone watching over you, even when you didn't want them to. Heck, I remember a time when Widow Burch saw me snitchin' some apples from the neighbor's tree. My momma knew before I took the first bite."

"That sounds good," Pete said. "Where I grew up, we didn't have any porches. And even if we had, I don't think anyone would've been sitting on them. The less you saw, the better off you were. And I'm not talking about kids stealing apples."

"That's a real shame," I said, taking a deep breath.

We sat in silence for a couple of minutes. The wind was still howling, pushing the clouds across the sky. "Strange night, ain't it?" Pete asked. "It's like the whole world is struggling with the Devil tonight."

Pete was right. Things just didn't feel the way they should. I could almost smell something evil in the air.

"Pete, what happened in there tonight?" I asked. "I feel like my insides have been ripped right out of me."

"Yeah," Pete said, trying to get comfortable. "That's kind of how I felt the first time I saw the boys like this. Only for me, it brought back memories of my own monsters. My old man was one mean dude. He'd come home drunk and beat me until I passed out."

I nodded in sympathy. "Yes, I know about your childhood." I said. "It must have taken years of counseling to get rid of those problems." How fortunate I had been. My dad had never been a drinking man.

"Not really," Pete said, rocking slightly on the edge of the steps. "I worked them out myself, little by little, over the years. But on nights like this, it seems as if those bad times happened just yesterday. You probably don't understand what I'm talking about, do you, Mel?"

"I can't rightly say I do," I answered, "but I want to understand."

"These kids are haunted by hideous creatures that stay hidden in the light of day, but as soon as night falls, they jump out," said Pete. "Maybe you can't sleep two or three times a year. Now and then you might have a nightmare that haunts you for a couple of days. Well, these kids battle for a good night's sleep every night. They fight, they run, they hide, and often they get caught by their nightmares. Most of the time they don't even remember what they dreamed about. It's as if they lead two separate lives, both equally real to them."

I could feel his pain. "What did you do to stop your nightmares, Pete?"

"Who says they've stopped? Over the years, things have gotten much better, but it wasn't until I started helping kids like these that I really began to heal. I'm not sure I'll ever heal completely."

"Pete, you're about the most level-headed person I know," I said. "It's hard to believe that you've been through some of the same terrors as my boys. What saved you?"

"An old man who used to live in my neighborhood," Pete said tenderly. "That old man taught me about the constellations, even had me believing that someday I might travel way up there among the stars." Pete pointed to the sky. "And who knows, maybe someday I will. This old guy—Crazy JJ, the kids called him—taught me about trees, birds, even let me keep a dog at his place. He wasn't crazy, not really. He was a believer, that's all. He believed in lost causes. Actually, Mel, you kind of remind me of him."

"Well, there sure are a lot of people who call me crazy. Sometimes, Pete, I think I am. I can't see that I'm making much of a difference to these boys. I'm no psychologist, and maybe that's what they need."

"Come on, Mel, aren't you listening to me? The boys don't need another psychologist." Pete shook his head. "They've had plenty of couch therapy. They need more 'Crazy JJ therapy'—more therapy sessions with chipmunks, cattle and horses. You know that trail-blazing you and the kids do every weekend? That's what they need. Psychologists? Give me a break, will ya?"

"You know, Pete, you're right," I said, resting my back against the wall of the cabin. "The media, the courts, CYS, the whole lousy bunch of them have me second-guessing myself."

"That's what they want you to do," Pete said, yawning. "But don't you fall prey to that gang of idiots. They have no idea what it's like dealing with these kids. Listen, do you for one minute think that the boys are going to go away from this place remembering the talks they had with their psychologists? I don't think so. You know what they're going to remember? Horseback rides, feeding the cattle, planting alfalfa. And they'll remember you, a man who cared when no one else did." Pete yawned again and scratched his shoulder.

"Thank you, Pete."

"For what?"

"For sharing the story about Crazy JJ and for telling me about yourself."

"Glad I could help," he said, standing up. "But next time you need to talk this late, stop by Cabin Two."

"Yeah," I laughed, "I'll do that. Go get some sleep. Goodnight, now."

Pete went inside, and in a couple of minutes all the lights were off. I was alone. I wished I could fall asleep. My day would be beginning in a few short hours, and by the look of things, I would be up to greet the dawn. By now the wind had died down, there was not a cloud left in the sky, and even the horses had quieted down. The moon shone bright. The shadows reappeared, motionless, but now they only looked like shadows.

I closed my eyes for a minute. What were these creatures that Pete was talking about, the creatures that robbed sleep from children and turned dreams into nightmares? Were they snakes hissing and spitting venom? Dragons breathing fire? Or were they parents trying to kill their children?

Cowards, all of them. I'd fight those creatures no matter what they looked like, and I'd take them down. I'd fight whatever evil terrified my boys. I'd march into hell to free those boys from the devils that plagued them.

I can't believe that I fell asleep with these thoughts squirming in my mind, but I must have, because the next thing I remembered, I was staring at a huge, burning cross. Sparks were shooting into the sky like fireworks on the Fourth of July. I tried to put the flames out with my hands but I couldn't. The flames were spreading to the right arm, and I couldn't stop them. No! I tried screaming, but I couldn't. I was frozen. The right arm of the cross burst into flames. No! No! That wasn't supposed to burn. The cross crumbled and fell to the ground. Only a pile of smoldering ashes remained. The sky was beginning to turn black as I searched through the ashes.

I gasped, waking myself.

I looked around for a moment, totally confused. Where was I? How did I get there? Was I still dreaming? I felt as if I had lost something. Yes, I did, and it was somewhere in the ashes. I looked down at my feet, expecting to see a pile of dying embers. What had I lost?

But there were no ashes, no cross. It was nothing more than a dream. No, it was more than a dream. It was a nightmare. My faith was lost in those ashes. That's what I was searching for and couldn't find. My greatest fear had showed itself to me while I slept. What if God turned away from me? What if I had to go through life without God's love and guidance? I shuddered, not from the damp night air, but from the thought of being alone. Lord, I prayed, do not forsake me.

A pale light appeared on the horizon. A cardinal chirped its wake-up call. I had made it through the night.

I had had a nightmare. I tried to convince myself that it was nothing more than that. But I still felt lost and alone. I had challenged the evil that plagued my boys, and it had entered my dreams. Who was there to help me, to fight for me, to take away my demons?

As I walked toward the farmhouse, struggling with my fears, I heard another scream. The lights in Cabin Two went on.

"Lord," I cried out loud. "Where are you?" I searched the morning sky, but there was no answer.

chapter fourteen
Daybreak

God enters by a private door into every individual.
Ralph Waldo Emerson

A S I W E N T about my business the next few days, I found I could barely function. I ate little, I was terse with the boys and the counselors, and I didn't even want to go riding. I looked to the Bible for comfort, but the moment I put my hand on its cover, I felt as if my fingers were on fire. The dream of the cross in ashes had shaken me to the very roots of my faith. Was it a sign that what I was doing was useless, that I was not doing the Lord's work but merely my own? I didn't quite know what to think.

TiAnda knew something was wrong and tried to get me to talk about what was happening to me, but I just couldn't tell her. I was tired, I said, I was run-down. The battle with the system was getting to me. While that was all true, I think she knew there was something more to my strange behavior than that. "Don't you miss church this Sunday," she advised me one evening. "I don't care what comes up. You've got to talk to Reverend Johnson."

Somehow I got through the next few days, though I don't remember getting a wink of sleep Friday or Saturday night. I just tossed and turned, seeing those ashes in my mind's eye and myself rooting through them. On Sunday morning I dressed, and drove TiAnda and some of the boys to church, but I might as well have been in a trance. The world felt cold and empty to me. Even the boys, with their happy chitchat and Sunday smiles, couldn't rouse me from the depths my spirit had fallen into. I entered the church that morning with tears in my heart, sure that God had forsaken me.

I didn't hear a word of the pastor's sermon, but after the church had emptied, TiAnda told me she was taking the boys to a nearby park and would come back for me soon. I just nodded; by then, tears were swimming in my eyes and I could barely see. *I don't belong here*, I thought to myself.

Once TiAnda left, I knelt down before the cross in front of the sanctuary. *If I am making a mistake, Lord, then just tell me so*, I prayed. I knelt there so long my knees became very stiff, but I would not move until I got a message. Suddenly I heard a voice. It said three words: "Son, it's Pa."

I was startled, thinking that Reverend Johnson had spoken to me, but I couldn't see anyone. Pale sunlight streamed through the stained glass windows, coloring the entire sanctuary in soft shades of blue, green, and violet. Had someone really spoken aloud? Or was the voice coming from my own heart? Then I knew.

The Lord is the Heavenly Father and Jesus Christ is His Son. But, in a way, I was also the Lord's child; he would guide me through my trials, as surely as my dad had led me on the road to being a man. *But even that wasn't all that those words meant*, I thought.

The Lord had showed me my mission, as clearly as if He had written me a letter, signed it, sealed it, and dropped it in the mail: I was a father, too, to many sons, not just Norris but to all the boys in the youth home, all those boys who needed a parent's love and guidance and support. And I had a father's responsibility toward them. "Son?" I felt a hand on my shoulder.

I leaped to my feet, nearly jumping out of my shoes. It

was the Reverend Johnson. He had come up behind me while I prayed. "You all right?" he asked. "Can I help you?"

I nodded, wiping my face with my handkerchief. "Yes, Reverend. I know this isn't exactly your line of work, but I want to tell you about something." As briefly as possible I told him about my troubling dream, the flaming cross, the crumbling embers, my frantic search. Reverend Johnson nodded.

"Mel, sometimes dreams mean a lot and sometimes they mean nothing, as you probably know. Does God send us all our dreams? No, I don't think He does. Satan is always lying in wait for all of us, trying to undo the Lord's good works and our faith in Him. That's what I think your dream is—evil's attempt to shake your faith. But the Lord smiles on you, Mel. Just look at the good you're doing those boys. Why, you're the father most of them never had."

I couldn't help but grin when he said that. "Yes, I believe you're right," I replied.

"You know, Mel, there's more than one way to interpret that dream of yours," said the pastor. "That fiery cross is not the cross of Christ; it's the cross of men, men with twisted morals and evil intentions. I should think you would be happy to watch that cross burn up. It's no wonder you didn't find anything in the ashes, because, Son, there's nothing to find—no goodness, no reason, no love, no faith—only hatred. But in good men, the Lord causes hatred to crumble into dust."

I nodded, too dumbstruck to speak. Suddenly I couldn't see my dream any other way: Of course it was not the Lord's cross. Christ's cross burned with passion and love, but it was never consumed.

That night I slept like a child in his father's arms.

chapter fifteen

Getting Caught in the System

There are only two places in our world where time takes precedence over the job to be done: school and prison.

William Glasser

W H E N   M O N D A Y   morning arrived, it felt more like Easter Sunday morning to me. I felt as if I had died and come back to life. Eager to begin my work around the youth home, I quickly showered and put on my three-piece navy pinstriped suit. I really didn't have to wear my Sunday clothes; a pair of old sweats would have done just fine, but somehow, I felt that this day called for my best. I began to take care of some paperwork that was in desperate need of being finished, and I did it with a smile. Now that certainly was progress on my part.

The buzz of the intercom interrupted my joyous morning. TiAnda picked up the phone. "It's Carol," she said, handing me the receiver.

"Yes, Carol," I said. "What's up?"

"You're needed in the office," she said in a tense voice and hung up.

"I have to go." I gave TiAnda a quick kiss and walked down to the trailer. I understood the meaning behind

145

Carol's tone of voice and wondered what kind of problem we were facing now.

"You know, Mel," Carol began, as soon as I walked in the door, "I hate always being the one to give you bad news. It seems as though it's become a part of my job around this place. But of all the bad news I've had to deliver, including the message from the Klan, this one's the hardest for me."

"What is it, Carol?" I asked, sitting down beside her.

"Richard has been suspended from school for having a BB gun in his locker."

"Damn!" I said. Richard, of all people. He was to be our shining example of what a difference we could make in our youth. He had everything going for him. "I can't believe this. It just doesn't make any sense. Richard? That doesn't sound like him."

"I know," Carol said, grabbing a box of tissues. Tears glistened in her eyes. "I asked the principal what Richard's explanation was for bringing the gun to school, but the principal didn't know. I don't think they even bothered to ask Richard why."

"What did the principal do?" I asked.

"He did what he called 'normal procedure.' He kicked Richard out of school. Richard's grandmother called here this morning, and she said she doesn't know where the boy is. She hasn't seen him since yesterday morning and was hoping that we had heard from him."

"Has Annie heard from him?" I asked.

"I doubt it, or she would have called by now. I knew it wouldn't work out if Richard moved in with his grand-mother. Didn't I tell you it wouldn't work?"

"Yes," I answered. "But it wasn't my decision to put Richard in the care of a woman who's almost ninety. You can thank the CYS for that."

"You know, Mel, they'll say it's not their fault for placing Richard with his grandmother. They'll say it was her fault for not taking proper care of the boy." Carol brushed a tear from her cheek.

"She didn't fail. The CYS did, and I'm getting real tired of those people not taking responsibility for their decisions. Who do they think they are, anyway?"

"Let's talk about this later." Carol said. "We need to concentrate on helping Richard right now."

"I know. So where should we start?"

"You go look for him," Carol said. "Here's his grandmother's address. You can start there."

"All right, I'll go," I promised. "Get Norris to cover for me."

I drove to Homewood, a forlorn, forgotten section of the city that had fallen into serious decay. The broken streets looked like a battleground in war-torn Beirut. Nearly every week there was a report of a drive-by shooting or drug bust.

After a half-hour search, I finally found the house. I rang the doorbell a couple of times before realizing that it probably hadn't worked in years. I pounded on the door, and when no one answered, I tried the door handle. To my surprise, it was unlocked. I opened the door and walked in. "Hello," I called.

"Who's there?" I heard a voice ask.

Richard's grandmother was making her way down the stairs, pinning up a few strands of her gray hair. "Oh, Mr. Blount, it's you. I was just about to change into my day clothes," she said. "It's early to be up and about, isn't it?"

"Well, ma'am, I think it's about ten o'clock. By the way, do you know that your door's unlocked?"

"It is? I thought I locked it last night. My memory's not what it used to be, Mr. Blount."

"Mrs. Robertson," I said, offering her my hand, "do you know where Richard is?"

"No, can't say that I do," she answered. "He could be up in his room. But when I looked there earlier, I didn't see him. He's been sneaking in and out since he came here to live. I don't know what's wrong with that boy. He don't listen very well to his grandma."

"You mind if I go take a look?"

147

"No, go right ahead. If he's up there, you tell him I don't want him leaving the house."

I ran up the steps and opened the door to Richard's bedroom. It was surprisingly neat and clean. The bed was made, and everything was put away except for one sock that hadn't quite made it all the way into the clothes hamper. But no Richard.

As I walked down the stairway, the front door opened.

"M–M–Mr. Mel," Richard said, standing in the doorway. "I thought that was your car. . . ."

"Where have you been?" I demanded.

"Out . . . out walkin' around," he stammered. "I guess you heard about me being kicked out of school, huh?"

"Yes," I answered. "That's why I'm here. I want to know why."

We walked out the door and sat on the porch steps. I looked around. Great front porch, but no rocking chair.

"Mr. Mel," Richard said, hanging his head low. "I didn't do nothing wrong. I wasn't up to no good, honest, I wasn't." Richard struggled to tell his side of the story. The confident young man who had left the youth home just a few months ago had fallen backward so fast that I could barely understand his words.

"I was only protectin' myself," he explained. "Some gang members from a different school beat me up a couple times, then the other day they threatened to kill me. And they meant it, too."

"Why were they going to kill you?"

"No reason I know of, Mr. Mel." Richard shrugged his shoulders. "They don't need no reason. They're a bad gang and they do pretty much whatever they like. That's a fact."

"Why didn't you tell your teachers?" I began to feel my head throbbing.

"Are you joking?" Richard asked. "If I told on them, those guys would kill me for sure."

"The police. Couldn't you tell them?"

"No way. The police ain't gonna spend time worrying

about me. We got people getting killed here every day. They don't care."

"Well, how about your social worker? Or me? Why didn't you tell me?"

"Hey, Mr. Mel," Richard said, looking at me for the first time. "I appreciate what you're sayin', but I ain't in the program anymore, remember? There ain't nothing you can do for me. Besides, out here you gotta learn to take care of yourself, and that's what I was doing. I ain't got no counselor anymore, except maybe on paper, 'cause I haven't seen one since I got back on the streets."

"I thought you had to report to your social worker once a week," I said, rubbing my head.

Richard didn't say anything. He just laughed.

I stared at the boy before me. Richard had won the heart of everyone at the youth home. There was such a simple honesty about him. It was hard to deal with the fact that we were losing him to a system in which schools didn't have the time to care and social workers did nothing but push paper and cash their paychecks.

"Mr. Mel," Richard said, looking me straight in the eye. "I wasn't gonna kill nobody. I just wanted to scare them, that's all. Sometimes if you act crazier than they are, they'll leave you alone. I know better than to kill someone."

"You mind your grandmother, you hear me, child?" I said. "Don't leave the house until they allow you back in school. You can't be getting yourself into any more trouble. You're in deep enough. I'm gonna talk to your grandmother about letting Annie see you." I stood up and arched my back. I was sore.

"Does Miss Annie and Miss Carol know about me?" Richard asked, looking up at me.

I nodded, rubbing the small of my back.

"Gee, I wish they didn't," Richard said, holding his head in his hands.

I spoke briefly with Richard's grandmother. I could tell she was desperate now, because she agreed to anything that we wanted to do.

Richard walked me to my car and shook my hand. "Thanks for comin' to see me, Mr. Mel. I wish I could go back to the youth home with you."

"So do I, Richard." I said. I looked at him standing on the crumbling sidewalk, waiting for me to rescue him, to take him where it was safe and no one would hurt him. But I couldn't. My hands had been tied by rules and regulations. *How ridiculous*, I thought. *Here's a boy begging for help, and I have to turn my back, get in my car and drive away.*

When I got back to the youth home, Norris and Carol were busy taking care of business. I went straight into my office and called Richard's principal on the phone.

"Mr. Blount," he said, "How can I help you?"

I explained Richard's situation and asked if we could meet to work something out.

"Well, I don't think a meeting will serve any real purpose," the principal said matter-of-factly. "I can appreciate your concern over this boy, but the situation is out of my hands. If a student brings a gun to school, he's out of here for a minimum of a week. The rules are very clear on this point. That's all there is to it."

"But," I argued, "in Richard's case, there are some extenuating circumstances that have to be taken into consideration."

"Excuse me, sir," the principal interrupted. "But every kid in this school who gets into trouble has a list of 'extenuating circumstances.' We can't handle those problems. Richard has a social worker and a grandmother to watch out for him. That's more than a lot of kids have. If they can't do their job and keep him in line, well, it's not my responsibility or the responsibility of my teaching staff to do the job for them. We simply do not have the time, the funding, or the manpower to take on everyone's problems. We're struggling just to teach the kids what the state requires.

"Mr. Blount, my job is to maintain order, and that's what I intend on doing. I can't risk having a kid killed on my school grounds."

"But," I pleaded, "maybe if we sit down and talk, we can make some special arrangements for Richard. The youth home is willing to assist you. If that means checking up on Richard every day. . . ."

"Maybe I'm not making myself clear. I can't make any special arrangements with you or the youth home. You don't have any authority over Richard."

"So what you're saying is 'too bad for Richard' because the system has failed him?"

"Listen, Mr. Blount," he said flatly. "You go do your job at the youth home and allow me to get back to running the school."

"So that's it?" I questioned, refusing to believe that we couldn't come to some kind of middle ground.

"I wish I could tell you differently. I really do," the principal said. His voice mellowed a bit. "But sometimes that's just the way things are. And you know what? Neither of us can change it."

"Well, sir, that's one more thing you and I don't agree on," I said. "If I felt I couldn't make this world a better place, I'd just stop living."

On one hand, I sympathized with the struggles of the educational system, especially a city school like Richard's. On the other hand, the injustices being committed against our children were intolerable. I pitied that principal. His cross had burned to the ground, and he didn't even know it.

I don't know how I made it through the rest of the day without crawling into some corner and falling asleep, but I did. As I was about to leave the office, Carol came in and actually had some good news for me.

"Annie and her husband will take Richard back to school as soon as his probation is over," Carol said. She seemed a little calmer about things. "They're going to meet with Richard's teacher and the principal and lay out a plan to keep better tabs on Richard's progress. Richard's grandmother has agreed to allow Richard to stay with Annie on the weekends. Annie said she would help Richard with his homework and make sure that he stays out of trouble."

"Has she actually talked to the principal?" I asked.

"No," Carol answered. "Annie's going to pay him a visit the day after tomorrow."

I started laughing. "I really feel sorry for him."

"Why?" Carol asked.

"If Annie nags him with the same energy she nags me about that library building, that poor guy doesn't stand a chance."

"I don't think that's funny."

"No, I guess you wouldn't." I walked out of the trailer and glanced across the field. For a minute, I thought I saw the new administration building. I needed some sleep.

When I got to the farmhouse, TiAnda greeted me in her blue silk evening dress. "Come on, babe," she said, ushering me down the hall. "Get ready. We have to be in Pittsburgh in less than an hour."

"What for?" I asked, pausing to look at my bed.

"For dinner, that's what." She said, shoving me into the bathroom. "You're the guest speaker, remember?"

No, I didn't remember.

"I can't believe you," TiAnda said, turning on the shower. "The church group is having a dinner, and you promised to talk."

"Oh, no. Can't Norris go?"

TiAnda pointed to the shower. "You'd rather babysit his kids?"

"You got a point there," I answered. "I'll be ready in fifteen minutes."

We drove into the city and got stuck in traffic at the Fort Pitt Tunnels. The cars crawled along like snails, and I struggled to keep myself awake. Finally, we made it to the church and had dinner. I made my speech, and just as we were on our way out the door, the pastor stopped us. Somehow he and TiAnda managed to convince me to drive to his place for dessert and coffee. And I don't even drink coffee.

We pulled up into our driveway at two in the morning.

By now I was feeling pretty numb. As TiAnda and I got out of the car, I saw Norris's porch light turn on.

"Dad, Dad," I heard him call. "Wait right there." Norris came running toward me in his slippers and bathrobe.

"What's wrong? Are the girls all right?" I asked, realizing that Norris would not be up this late unless something were terribly wrong. *Oh, Lord*, I thought, *it's my momma*.

"No, no," he said, "it's nothing like that, but we do have some awful trouble. Richard was a passenger in a stolen car. The police are holding him at Station House Five in Homewood."

I didn't ask any questions. I just got back into my car and headed back toward Pittsburgh. I didn't know what good I'd be able to do, but I knew I had to try to do something.

I sat in a cold, stark room at the police station, waiting for them to bring Richard to me. Richard was in such deep trouble this time that I was afraid my rope would not reach him.

"Mr.–Mr. Mel." Richard was scared. His stammering was uncontrollable. "I didn't steal the car. No, sir. I was only riding in it. That's the truth, Mr. Mel. You gotta believe me. Gerry stole the car. Not me. I'm not that stupid."

"What were you doing in the car in the first place?" I asked, closing my eyes for a second. I heard his answer, but it didn't register in my brain right away.

"You don't know?" I asked, rubbing my eyes. " 'I don't know' is not an acceptable answer, Richard. I'm too tired to listen to this. You give it to me straight, you hear me? If you don't, I'm leaving right now."

"No! Don't go, Mr. Mel. It was like this, okay? I was just walking around the streets when this kid, Gerry, pulls up in a nice car and asks me if I want to go for a ride. I said, 'Sure, why not?' and got in. It wasn't any big deal."

"Where did you think he got the car?" I asked.

"I don't know. I guess I thought he'd borrowed it."

153

"Did you ask him?"

"No, sir. Why should I? He was good enough to offer me a ride. I didn't want to insult the guy."

"Did it occur to you that the car could be stolen? After all, Richard, it was a brand-new Saab."

"Honest, Mr. Mel, I didn't even think about it. All I knew was that I had nowhere to go and nothin' to do. So I went for a ride. I didn't harm nobody. I wasn't looking for any trouble."

"Well, I'm not sure where we go from here," I said, rubbing the top of my head. "From what the police tell me, they're going to take you to Grandville in the morning."

"Prison? You can't let them take me there!" Richard shouted, jumping out of his chair and knocking it over.

"It's not prison, it's juvenile hall. It's only for a couple of days until they find another place for you," I explained. "Richard, the car you were in was the same car used during the robbery of a convenience store earlier this evening. If they find out you had anything to do with that robbery, nothing I say or do is going to help you."

"I wasn't in no hold-up. That Gerry's crazy." Richard was once again the frightened boy who had showed up at the youth home almost two years ago. He was slipping away from me.

"Now you settle yourself," I said, grabbing hold of his arms.

"I know you're real scared, but you're going to have to cooperate, understand? You can't afford to do anything to get yourself into more trouble. The charges against you are very serious. I want you to do everything they tell you, and I'll see what I can do for you." I gave him a quick hug. Richard was crying as the police and social worker escorted him down the hall. I watched as they disappeared behind a steel door and felt my heart drop as I heard the door slam shut.

For the second time in eight hours, I was driving back to Taylorstown from the city. As I was leaving Pittsburgh, rush hour was just beginning. I hoped that TiAnda had a very light day planned for me.

As I walked in the door, TiAnda held the phone out to me. "It's Annie."

Annie took the news about Richard the way I expected. Badly.

"This whole system stinks!" Annie shouted into the phone. "They're going to lock him up. I just know they will. Mel, what are we going to do?"

"I don't think there's anything we can do, but I'll talk to the judge at Richard's hearing. Maybe he can do something."

"Do you honestly think it will help?" Annie said, sobbing.

"Honestly?"

"Yes, honestly. Don't start pulling punches with me now."

"I think Richard's headed for a stay in Grandville. I think it's best you just forget about ever getting custody of him. You'll fall in love with some other little kid, and things will turn out differently." There was a long silence. "Annie, are you still there?"

"Sorry," Annie answered. "I'm just tired of this whole thing. I really don't know how you keep going on. I just can't believe that Richard was only a few days away from getting his life back in order."

"Sometimes it just doesn't make any sense, no matter how many ways you try to figure it," I said, struggling to keep my eyes open. "The Lord has His own way of making everything work out. You've got to believe that."

"Well, believing sure is hard at times," Annie said. "But I suppose that I have to believe, just like you do."

The sun was beginning to shine through the blinds as I hung up the phone. *I'm getting to old for this all-night stuff*, I thought.

"Come on, honey," TiAnda said. "I'll cancel all your morning appointments. Go get some sleep."

"Thank you, baby, thank you." I undressed, crawled

155

into bed, stretched, yawned, and closed my eyes, but I couldn't sleep. What was I going to do about Richard?

He knows every star in the vast heavens and calls them by name. I kept hearing that phrase in my mind, though I couldn't remember where it came from. I figured it was the Lord's way of telling me that He wouldn't forget Richard. But just in case He let one star slip by, I vowed to remind God of Richard every night. Somewhere between the thoughts of Richard and the stars, I finally fell asleep.

chapter sixteen

The Accusation

A reputation once broken may possibly be repaired, but the world will always keep their eyes on the spot where the crack was.

Joseph Hall

"D A D! D A D!" I heard Norris shouting to me in my dream. I could hear him, but I couldn't see him. A panic seized me. He must be in trouble. I called back to him. "Dad! Dad!" I heard him call again. Where was he?

Suddenly I woke with a start. Norris was standing by the bed, looking down at me. "Norris, where have you been?"

"I've been in the office. You must have been dreaming."

"What time is it?" I squinted at the alarm clock.

"About nine-thirty."

I reached for my glasses and glanced at the clock. "Try nine."

"Okay, nine," he said.

"Morning or evening?" I asked.

"Morning."

"I've only had two hours of sleep. What are you trying to do, kill me?"

"I'm sorry, Dad, but you have a big meeting this

morning at ten. You promised some businessmen a private tour of the place, remember? They're thinking about donating some money to the home," Norris explained, as he handed me my bathrobe. "We sure could use the money."

I couldn't remember, but if Norris was dragging me out of bed, it must be so. "How 'bout if you cover for me?"

"I can't take this one, Dad. It's too important. Now c'mon, go shower up. I'll make you some breakfast." Norris turned and walked toward the door. "You know, Dad, you ought to take some time off. You really look terrible."

Well, that was just what a man who hadn't slept in three days and who was about to conduct an important meeting needed to hear.

Norris and I talked briefly about Richard's situation, and we both agreed to speak on Richard's behalf at the court hearing. "I don't think it'll make any difference," Norris sighed. "He's up on criminal charges."

This day was not getting off on the right track. I was barely able to think straight. I just wanted to sleep. And to make matters worse, I was coming down with a cold.

The meeting went on until noon. After the visitors drove away, I stopped into the office for a few minutes just to look over the mail. I really didn't care what else was planned for me—I was on my way to bed.

A registered letter from the County Common Pleas Court in Pittsburgh was sitting on top of the pile of mail. At first, I thought another one of our boys had gotten into trouble and this was a summons for a youth-home representative to be present at the court hearing. I was partly right. It was a summons to appear in court but not on behalf of one of the boys.

In disbelief, I read the summons over and over. I read it out loud. I read it to myself. Then I walked over to the trash can and threw it out. Before stepping away, I kicked the can and sent it sailing across the room.

"What's going on in here?" Carol asked, walking into the office.

"That!" I pointed to the overturned container that was still trembling in the corner.

"You're upset about a little garbage?" Carol wrinkled her forehead.

"No. Yes. Here." I pulled the summons out of the trash. "Read this."

Carol scanned the summons. "Oh, no!" she gasped. "I can't believe it. This is absolutely the most ridiculous. . . ."

"It's more than ridiculous," I interrupted, taking the summons from her hand and throwing it toward the overturned can. "It's, it's . . ."

"Evil?"

"Good word," I agreed. I sat down in my chair. What did I do to deserve this?

"Well, what are you going to do?" Carol asked, sitting down beside me. "We all know it just isn't true. No one's going to believe this. I think you better call your lawyer."

"I'll do it later," I said, standing up. I reached down and picked up the summons from the floor. "I'm going for a ride. The Lord and I have to talk."

My mind was racing as fast as Wind as she galloped up the hillside. I arrived at my mountaintop and stared out over Taylorstown. The town was quiet and peaceful-looking. Smoke rose from a few chimneys as a yellow school bus carried children home from school. Everything appeared to be in order, but that was far from the truth.

"Okay, Lord," I whispered. "I'm not saying that I need to know the reasoning behind what you decide. I don't need to know every turn and twist in the road. I'm used to traveling without a map. And you know I don't do much complaining. If you tell me to start walking, I walk. Now, you know that's true, Lord. But this," I said, waving the paper in the air, "This is pretty hard for me to take. Why am I being sued for child abuse?"

I looked around for a sign. There were no birds. No branches. No whispers in the wind. I waited a bit longer. Nothing.

"Okay, Lord," I said rather loudly as I dismounted and

walked back and forth across the summit. "I know that I can't measure your time by my watch. I'll be patient." I felt so angry I could hit something. Instead I took my hat from my head and pitched it as far as I could over the hillside. "Lord, I'm trusting that your purpose will be known to me. If you decide not to tell me, well, I guess I just don't need to know."

I glanced toward the woods and, oddly enough, even up here I had an audience. A few of the neighbor's workers were standing near the fence at the edge of the woods, watching me. Now for sure they would think I was crazy.

I got back on Wind, and with a leap she took off galloping down the hillside. "Whoa, girl," I called to her, pulling on the reins. "Wrong way." She went a little farther, then stopped with a jerk. "Oh, yeah, thanks." I patted her, dismounted, and picked up my hat. That horse was smarter than a lot of people I knew.

Slowly, Wind headed for the farmhouse, giving me time to think. My thoughts were scattered, but one thing I knew for certain: I had never abused my boys, no matter what anyone said. And no one was going to stop me or the youth home from doing our job. I felt as though I had been kicked in the stomach. It took my breath away temporarily, but I would recover. I just needed some sleep, then I would be able to breathe a little easier.

As I neared the home, I noticed a large rental truck parked in front of Cabin One. *Oh, great,* I thought. The bank was probably repossessing the place. It wouldn't have surprised me. That's just the way things seemed to be going lately.

I rode up to the truck and saw Annie and her husband in the back. "What's going on?" I asked.

"Books," Annie said, pointing to the boxes. "Roughly two thousand of them. This was supposed to be a surprise. But you know, Mel, with Richard in trouble, I'm not as happy about the books as I should be."

"Where in creation did you get all of this?" I was amazed. "Where are we going to put it?"

"In Cabin One. We can build some shelves and make ourselves a temporary library. I've already raised the money and marked off an area in the basement. It's better than nothing."

"Yeah, okay, but where did you get the books?" I asked again.

"From the generous people of Pittsburgh." Annie turned and joined her husband. They both picked up a box and headed down the ramp. "Oh, before I forget . . . vans are coming from Ohio and West Virginia. They're donating books, too."

"Do you have any idea how many books we're going to have?" I asked, not sure I wanted to hear the answer.

"Altogether? Around five thousand," Annie answered. "Five thousand little keys to unlock the mind. Dreams, travel, inspiration, and all for free."

Maybe this wasn't really happening. Maybe I was dreaming. *No, this isn't a dream*, I thought, as I saw three vans drive up the road toward the youth home. If I hadn't been so tired, I would have helped them unload. What a wonderful show of support! It was good to know that somebody, somewhere, still believed that I was doing the right thing.

As I was brushing down Wind, Norris entered the barn and stood silently watching me. From the look on his face, I guessed he had heard the bad news from Carol.

"Well?" he finally said. "What do you make of all this?"

"To tell you the truth, Son, I can't get my mind to focus for more than a few seconds at a time. Can we talk about this later?"

"I'll tell you what I think," Norris continued, as if he hadn't heard. "I think someone is trying to shut us down. Know why? 'Cause you're a black man taking care of troubled kids, and the program you have is succeeding. They never thought you'd actually get this place to work."

"Why not?" I could see that we were going to have this discussion whether I was coherent or not.

161

"Because their programs don't work. And they're the ones with the degrees, the little stamps of approval from the system that say, 'Now you're allowed to help a child.' You're confusing them, Dad. They think black ex-football players aren't supposed to be any good at working with children."

Norris stopped talking just long enough to take a deep breath. "Maybe the Klan's involved. I'll bet they are. And if it isn't the Klan, then it's someone who thinks like them. If every racist wore a white robe, at least we would know what we're up against."

"Let's not get into all that now," I said, leading Wind into her stall. "I'll call my attorney. Maybe things aren't as bad as we think they are. Have any of the newspapers called about this?"

"No, but they will." Norris picked up a piece of fresh straw and began chewing on it. "You can mark my words, the Legal Aid Society and CYS won't keep this to themselves. If they're gonna hang you, they'll need the help of a newspaper."

"I don't know," I said. I felt a little calmer now that I'd had a chance to think about it. "The CYS and Legal Aid Society might be satisified just to bring me before a judge. Maybe they just want me to change a few things around here to fit their rules. We'll have to wait and see."

"Well, as much as I would like to believe that," said Norris, "I still say it's going to get worse . . . much worse."

• • •

It began snowing as I drove to my eight o'clock court hearing. The weather report called for ten to twelve inches. The traffic reacted badly to the snowfall, moving slowly through the tunnel, across the bridge and into the city. I glanced at my watch. If I didn't have trouble finding a parking space, I would just make it in time.

I was prepared to go before the judge. I didn't have anything to hide. I had had a week to think about the charges the CYS and Legal Aid Society were bringing against me, and I was sure that I had done nothing that could be considered child abuse. The judge would see that, my attorney assured me.

I parked in a garage, dusted the snow off my Stetson, and walked into the lobby of the courthouse. My attorney, Paul Garrison, was waiting for me.

"You look pretty awful," he said, reaching out to shake my hand. "You should take a vacation."

"I've had some trouble sleeping lately, and now I have this darn cold," I said, wiping my nose with a tissue. "Since I started this youth home, I've had lots of colds. I think every time the kids get sick, so do I."

"Yeah, last year I caught the chicken pox from my boy," Paul said. He had me wondering for a moment if I ever had the chicken pox, and I made a mental note to ask my momma.

We stepped into the elevator and rode to the fifth floor. Adrienne Forte, the lawyer from the Legal Aid Society, was taking a drink from the fountain, and I walked by her unnoticed. A few social workers from CYS, standing around talking, ignored me as I walked by. Then I noticed Sally standing in a corner—Sally, the counselor we had fired a few months ago.

"I suppose she's not a witness for the defense," I whispered to Paul.

"You're right about that," Paul answered. "In fact, she's the only witness for the prosecution."

The judge was late. With the snow and traffic the way they were, that wasn't surprising. Finally he arrived, and we filed into the courtroom.

I was pleasantly surprised to see that none of the media was present. I must have been correct when I guessed that the Legal Aid Society and CYS didn't want this to turn into a circus. *Or*, I thought, *they know the truth and know they don't have a case. But then, why are they doing this?* I would soon find out.

We all stood when Judge Straussman entered the

courtroom. The judge and the court clerk exchanged a few words, then the judge called my name.

"Mr. Blount," Judge Straussman began. "Have the charges being brought against you been explained to you by your attorney?"

"Yes, Your Honor," I answered.

"Do you understand them?"

"Yes, Your Honor."

"Then let's proceed. Keep in mind, Mr. Blount, that this is a hearing to determine what action, if any, will be taken against you. The Legal Aid Society has yet to prove their case. You will be allowed plenty of time to tell your side. I want to keep this informal so that you or your attorney may ask questions as we proceed. Mr. Blount, if you don't understand something, let us know."

"Yes, Your Honor."

The games began. I listened to what seemed to be an endless stream of accusations. I had no idea where they had gotten their information.

"And, Your Honor," said Ms. Forte, "I must once again remind you that Mr. Blount was warned last year to stop paddling the boys."

"Mr. Blount," the judge said, turning toward me. "That was Legal Aid's case. What would you like to say on your behalf?"

My attorney talked first for about five minutes, then he turned to me. "Mel, why don't you say something now?"

"Your Honor," I said, clearing my throat, "I'm going to make this short. I admitted that last year I paddled two of my boys, but I never beat them. When the Legal Aid Society told me that the state did not allow what they call 'corporal punishment,' I didn't do it again, that is, until the time with James Baldwin. James was being real bad. He had been warned time and again, but he didn't listen. If Miss Nancy over there remembers—she was his caseworker—we told her that the disciplinary procedures that the state wanted us to use weren't working. Well, sir, I finally decided to spank him, and I did."

"Did his behavior improve, Mr. Blount?" the judge asked.

"Yes, Your Honor, we haven't had a problem since. You see, sir, these kids are troubled. They're good, but they have problems. I'm just about their last hope. When I discipline them by making them clean out the barn or work in the fields, I'm teaching them self-discipline—you do something out of line and you got to pay. I show them that I care enough to take the time to make sure they aren't getting away with anything. These kids have been allowed to take the easy way out for a long time. Well, sir, not at the Mel Blount Youth Home.

"Your Honor, I admit we broke some rules. I know that I made some mistakes, but whatever those mistakes were, Mel Blount is not about abusing children. If I wanted to beat up on little kids, I'm sure I could have found a way that was a darn sight cheaper and easier than starting up a youth home.

"I know of at least one time that a counselor made a boy take underwear smeared with manure and wear it on his head. I wasn't involved with that punishment and I don't condone such treatment. That particular counselor is no longer with us.

"And this horse-trailer thing. Judge, the only time-out rooms we have are in the cabins. Once we did put one of the boys into a horse trailer to calm him down. I'm talking about a real nice trailer, not dirty, not smelly. Nice and clean. The boy was out of control, and that's nothing new around the youth home. Sometimes these boys just snap. Most of the time, we don't even know what sets them off. Well, anyway, the counselor had to use the handiest space to confine the boy before he hurt himself or one of the other boys.

"The Legal Aid Society and the CYS have also told you I'm understaffed. There's no doubt about that. I am. The counselors I have are underpaid and overworked. Money is a big problem at the home. And I don't see how that problem's gonna get fixed any time soon. We had some real bad press lately. The media made it look like I was running a boot camp, and our supporters backed off. But I'm not belly-aching. We'll manage.

"Your Honor, we've broken some rules, and if that's against the law, then I'm truly sorry. But I'm telling you again, we don't abuse the boys, and the Legal Aid Society and the CYS know that.

"I believe there's something more to these accusations. I mean, the Legal Aid Society and CYS know they don't have a case for abuse. I believe they've known that all along.

"I have one more thing to say and then I'll shut up. My program is a good one. And if given enough time and support, I'll prove it to you. I'm only asking that the Legal Aid Society and CYS work with us, help us. But I got to be real honest, Your Honor. We at the youth home are in the front trenches every day, fighting to save these kids. We are the doers. They," I said, pointing across the table to my accusers, "are the rule-givers. The overseers. And there's nothing wrong with that. We need both. Surely there's a middle ground between the two of us. After all, we have to put the children first, not ourselves. That's all I have to offer in my defense, Your Honor."

We took a short recess. While the judge was deciding my fate, Paul and I made small talk about the court building, the fact that the city of Pittsburgh was finally putting up street signs, and the possibility of a Steeler comeback. We liked the architecture, were grateful for the signs, and didn't think the Steelers had a rat's chance at a cat convention.

Finally we were called back into the courtroom.

'I've listened carefully to both sides and, frankly, I'm troubled myself," Judge Straussman began. "I'm troubled because I see before me a man who is working hard to do good. He's doing something that we all should be doing, helping our youth. But he's also a man who has admitted that, in caring for the children, he committed acts that are against the law where the treatment of children in govern-ment-funded programs are concerned. I fully understand why Mr. Blount did what he did. Probably most parents, at one time or another, have resorted to spanking their children when all else failed. Does that make them guilty of child abuse? I don't believe so. Furthermore, I don't believe that Mr. Blount is guilty of malice or abuse.

"Yet the law is the law and, Mr. Blount, it appears that you have broken the law. Child Youth Services and the Legal Aid Society are taking you to task on these points. They have made their position very clear. While I think they may have gone a little overboard in their attempt to enforce the rules, that is their right.

"First, I'm recommending that you hire more qualified counselors. And, sir, see to it that you do the necessary background check on all of them. Also, be sure to document the training procedures you have put them through. Second, you must refrain from any further corporal punishment. Third, I want you to work with CYS and the Legal Aid Society. Establish a time-out room and use it. Make sure your counselors know the rules. Is that understood, Mr. Blount?"

"Yes, Your Honor," I answered.

"Now as far as you people at CYS and the Legal Aid Society are concerned, I understand your accusations, and you have made your intentions clear to me. I feel that I have adequately addressed them. Mr. Blount is aware of his program's deficiencies, and he is willing to work to improve things. He has a fine program, so I want you to cooperate with him. Take the necessary steps to get this youth home back on track.

"You will prepare a consent order that will address how the problems will be corrected and submit it to Mr. Blount within two weeks. Then, Mr. Blount, you will sign it. While I don't see any one thing that is serious in nature, there are enough problems to warrant some fixing up.

"Once again, I want cooperation here. I'll be keeping a close eye on this, so please make it work."

When I left the courtroom, I felt a little better. I knew that the problems the home was having could be fixed, but where was I going to get the money? Every recommendation was going to cost us.

As I walked down Grant Street on my way to the parking garage, a car was spinning its wheels on the snow-covered road. The wheels finally grabbed the pavement, sending the car flying into the intersection, where it almost collided with another car. *What a mess*, I thought. *Winter in Pennsylvania—I probably would never get used to it.*

A man was leaning against the wall of one of the office buildings, a sign dangling from his neck: "I'm hungry and homeless, please help." I walked over to him and pointed to a fast-food restaurant on the corner. "Come with me. I'll buy you some food."

"No, sir," he said, shaking his head wildly. "Just give me the money, and I'll buy my own food."

"I'd rather you let me buy it," I said. "Go in there and order whatever you like. I'll pay for it."

He glared at me and spat on my boots. "Aw, get outta here, nigger." I was taken aback for a few seconds, then walked away as he hollered a stream of curses at me.

chapter seventeen

Bad News Travels Fast

There is so much good in the worst of us and so much bad in the best of us, that it hardly becomes any of us to talk about the rest of us.

Anonymous

T H E   D R I V E   back to the youth home took twice as long as it usually did. The roads were slippery, the wind had picked up, and the youth-home minivan was rocking back and forth.

I didn't have time to think about the hearing because what little concentration I had left went into driving. My cold was getting worse, and I thought I had a fever.

Finally, I turned onto the youth home's road, fishtailing my way up. The kids stopped playing long enough to watch my struggle, waving and cheering when I made it to the top and parked.

I stomped the snow off my boots, then entered the trailer.

"So?" Carol said, staring at me. "When are you going to jail?"

I smiled. "Actually, it went pretty well. The judge was fair, and best of all, the CYS and Legal Aid Society's accusations didn't hold water."

"I knew they wouldn't," Carol said, handing me my

phone messages. "You had a call from some guy down at the Allegheny County referral office. I asked him what it was about, but he said he wanted to talk to you directly. I think, before you call it a day, you should call the man. Maybe they want to send another child here. And, Mel, you don't look good. You should get some rest."

I opened my desk drawer and searched around for some aspirin. The bottle was empty. I didn't need an aspirin anyway. I needed a doctor.

I dialed the number of the county official.

"Mr. Blount," the man on the other line said. "I'm glad you returned my call. I had a call from the Department of Public Welfare today. They have decided that we should stop referring children to the youth home. I wouldn't worry about it, though. It's just a temporary thing. This stuff happens."

"Do you care to explain why they've decided to stop sending kids here?" I asked, feeling none too friendly.

"Well, the Department of Public Welfare has to investigate the home. It's normal procedure to investigate any charges of child abuse."

"I thought that's what my court hearing was all about." I said, growing very impatient.

"Yes, but the Department of Public Welfare has to do its own investigation," he explained. "From what I've been told, the department is looking into abuse, ridicule, and humiliation."

"Do you mind if I ask you a couple of questions?"

"Go on, shoot," he answered.

"Where are they going to put the boys that were scheduled to come here next week? Back on the streets? In Grandville? Where?" '

"Hey, Mr. Blount," he said, "I'm only the messenger. This wasn't my decision. Off the record, I don't have any problem with what you're doing, but I don't have a vote. The CYS started this, not me."

"Well, how long do you think the investigation is going

to take?" I tried to take a deep breath but couldn't. I started coughing.

"You sound pretty bad, Mr. Blount," the young man said. "You should see a doctor."

"How long?" I asked again.

"I don't know."

"Guess. One week? Five weeks? Ten years?" I said. My patience was gone.

"Like I said, I'm only the messenger. But there's a bit of good news in all of this," he said cheerfully. "You can keep the boys that are already there."

That was it. I was mad. "You mean to tell me. . . ." I coughed into the phone, ". . . that I can't be trusted with any new kids, but I can be trusted with the ones that are here? That's about the stupidest thing I've ever heard."

"Yeah, I hear you," the young man said, sighing deeply. "Doesn't make much sense, does it? But Mr. Blount, we don't make the rules."

I hung up the phone and blew my nose. "Lord, I'm getting tired," I whispered. I reached for the tissue box. Darn, out of tissues.

"Hey, Dad," Norris said, poking his head in the door. "What do you say to spending some time with your son? I thought a ride through the snow would be fun."

Of course, Norris would decide to bond with his poor, sick dad in the middle of a snowstorm. "Okay, a short ride."

"Great. Change your clothes, and I'll meet you in the barn."

By the time I'd changed, Norris had saddled Wind and Tomahawk, a black gelding, and led them to the front door. We mounted and rode off across the snowy meadows. Soon, despite my cold, I began having a good time. The air felt good. Norris and I talked and laughed. Strangely enough, he never asked me about the trial.

We were heading back to the barn when Norris suddenly brought Tomahawk to a halt. "Do you recognize that guy standing outside the fence?" Norris called.

"No," I answered, shaking my head. "I can't tell who he is, but I think that's Tony with him, isn't it?"

"Yeah, that's Tony, all right. Why isn't that kid playing with the other boys? Didn't you warn him about talking to strangers?"

"Yes," I answered, urging Wind into a trot. "Let's go check it out."

As we neared the fence, the man looked over at us and quickly ran into the nearby woods.

"Should I go after him?" Norris asked, getting ready to dismount. "He should be easy to track in the snow."

"No, let him go," I answered. "For all we know, he may have a gun and decide to use it."

What's going on around this place? I asked myself. Maybe it was nothing. Maybe it was just some man taking a walk in the woods. Maybe he saw the boys and stopped to talk with one of them. It was probably all very innocent. Who was I kidding? Innocence doesn't run.

"Am I in trouble, Mr. Mel?" Tony asked, as I reached down and lifted him onto my saddle.

"What do you think?" I asked. My head was beginning to throb.

"I think I'm in trouble," he said, scrunching up his face.

"And why is that?" I asked, as Wind trotted toward the barn.

"Because you told me not to talk to strangers. But, Mr. Mel, this guy really wasn't a stranger. I talked to him a couple of times."

"Oh, you did? When?"

"At the youth home," he answered. "He was with a bunch of people. Remember when everyone came to look at the cabins? It was then. And I saw him at the Christmas party. He said he was a guest."

Oh, him, I thought. "If he were a guest, why do think you got in trouble for talking to him?"

"Oh, yeah. I didn't think about that," Tony replied, adjusting himself in the saddle.

"What do you and this guy talk about?"

"Well, he asks me a lot of questions," Tony answered, still not understanding the gravity of the situation. "Like how's the food here, do I like the counselors. Do I like you. He wanted to know if you ever hit me."

"And do you like the food?"

"Yessir," he quickly answered.

"The counselors?" I asked, as we dismounted and entered the barn.

"I like most of the counselors," he said, helping me hang the saddle on a peg. "I really like Mr. Pete. He's my favorite. I like you, too, Norris.

"I'll tell you who I don't like, though. Miss Susan. I never heard a woman yell as much as she does. You know, once she grabbed me by the collar and made me stand in the corner with my face to the wall. I didn't even do anything."

"Wasn't that the time you threw a piece of meat at Henry?" I asked, rubbing Wind down with an old towel.

"Well, yeah, but Henry kicked me under the table first and nothing happened to *him*," Tony defended himself.

"Sometimes life's unfair," Norris said, looking at me. "But. . . ." Norris grabbed Tony and lifted him into the air. "That doesn't mean you throw meat in someone's face." Tony laughed and scrambled to break loose from Norris's grasp. The two of them played around while I finished brushing down the horses.

"So what did you tell that guy about me?" I asked.

Tony walked over to me and smiled. For a moment I thought an angel was standing in front of me, he looked so innocent. Then he tried to sugar-talk me. "I told him if it weren't for you, I'd still be on the streets. Heck, I might even be dead by now. I told him you're in the Hall of Fame for one reason—'cause you're the best. I said to the guy, 'Mr. Mel never hit me or anything.' "

"Well, thank you for saying those things." I patted him on the back. "Now, I want you to clean out the stables," I said, pointing to a mess one of the horses had just made. "Then you're on restriction for a week."

Tony nodded. He didn't bother to put up a fight.

"Mr. Mel," Tony called, as Norris and I were leaving the barn. "That guy told me to call him if you hit any of the kids. He gave me his phone number, but I lost it. The guy said sometimes you do things to us boys that you're not supposed to do."

I felt a shiver go through my body. For a moment I saw the little boy at the cross-burning. How easy it is to manipulate children and plant seeds of mistrust in their young minds. A few words of deceit disguised as concern and caring can cripple a child for life. My boys didn't need anyone feeding them this stuff; they'd already had enough damage done to them.

"You keep away from that guy," I warned. "If he ever comes around here again, you come and get me or Norris. We'll answer his questions."

"Sure, Mr. Mel," he said, picking up a shovel. "You don't have to tell me twice."

• • •

Later that evening, as TiAnda and I were about to sit down to dinner, I told TiAnda about the reporter. "Oh, that reminds me," she said. Her face suddenly looked frightened. "Annie called last night and asked me to tell you that some reporter called her. He said you had told him to call. Annie said he was pretty nasty, so she hung up on him. Mel, please tell me—what's going on?"

"I wish I knew," I said, picking up the salt shaker.

"Oh, no. Too much sodium." TiAnda took the salt from my hand. "Do you think it has something do to with the court hearing?"

"No, my guess is that something else is going on here."

We finished eating, and I went into the living room to rest. Just as I was getting comfortable, the phone rang.

"Toopie! Sis, how are you?" If there was one person who could cheer me up, it was Toopie.

"Mel, you sound awful," she said. "You're not taking

care of yourself. It's those Pennsylvania winters. I keep telling you to move back to Georgia."

"Can't say that isn't a tempting thought," I said, stretching out on the couch. "So how's everything?"

"Not good, I'm afraid." I could hear the tension in her voice. "Momma called me a few minutes ago, and I can tell something has her real upset."

"Oh, Lord, what's wrong?"

"I don't know. She wouldn't tell me. I know she had a doctor's appointment today. Maybe he gave her some bad news," Toopie explained. "But I have a hunch it's more than that, because when I mentioned your name, she started to cry. Do you have any idea what could be wrong?"

"I haven't talked to Momma since last week," I answered.

"Mel, I'm not in Savannah. I'm at a conference in Dallas, so I can't drive up and find out what's troubling her. She called my house and George gave her my number. For some reason, she didn't want me to call her.

"I think you ought to go down and visit her for a couple of days. Maybe she's just worrying about you. You know, you being the baby and all."

"Okay, I'll call you from home," I said, sitting up. My head was pounding. "I'll leave tomorrow morning."

I hung up with Toopie and dialed my momma. No answer. I waited ten minutes and dialed again. Still no answer.

"Mel," TiAnda said, watching me pace back and forth across the living room. "Have Clint go over and check on your mom if you're that worried about her."

I picked up the phone and dialed Clint. No answer. I tried Momma again. "She's there, TiAnda. Toopie talked with her a few minutes ago. I just don't know why she isn't answering."

chapter eighteen
The Trip South

One very important ingredient of success is a good, wide-awake, persistent, tireless enemy.

Frank B. Shutts

T H E   T R I P   to Georgia was uneventful except for TiAnda's reaction to her sick husband's refusal to stay in bed. But I told her that if I didn't make this trip and something happened to my momma, I would never be able to forgive myself. Although it was probably nothing to worry about, I didn't want to take any chances.

I arrived just before dusk, half expecting to see my momma sitting in her rocking chair on the front porch. When she wasn't there, I felt a surge of panic rush through me. I threw the car into park and ran into the house calling, "Momma! Momma!"

"I'm in here, Son," she called. "I'm in the kitchen."

I ran into the kitchen and saw her bent over the stove, taking a pie out of the oven. "Look what I baked for you," she said, turning around and smiling. "Your favorite— sweet potato pie."

"How did you know I was coming to visit, Momma?" I asked, looking around the kitchen. There was a freshly baked ham on the counter, greens cooking on the stove, a loaf of homemade bread on the table, and fried chicken piled up on a platter.

"Clint told me," she answered.

"How did Clint know?"

"Toopie told him." She smiled and reached out her arms for me. "You come over here and let me greet my son proper." As she took a step toward me, I noticed her limp slightly. I gave her a big hug and helped her into a chair. "How's your foot, Momma?"

"My circulation has gone and slowed down," she said. "Those things start happenin' when you get old. The doctor gave me some medicine and said I would be fine. I just got to remember to take my pills and soak my foot a couple times a day."

"You sit right down and don't you lift another finger," I said. See? I told myself, nothing's wrong. Her foot's not too bad. She just missed me, that's all. "Momma, you didn't have to go to so much trouble." I said, looking again at all the food. "It smells great." I bent down and gave her a kiss. Actually, I was so congested, I couldn't smell a thing. "I'm gonna have a great big piece of pie right now." I just hoped my stomach would hold it down.

"No, honey, it's got to cool some," she started to stand up. "I'll just stick it out on the porch for a few minutes."

"No you don't," I said, grabbing a potholder. "I can do that. You just stay put. I swear you just don't know how to kick back and relax."

I walked out on the porch and placed the pie on the railing. That worn railing had held a lot of pies in its day. The place was beginning to show its age. When the family house where my parents had raised their eleven kids had burned to the ground, Momma didn't care much where she lived. She moved into this small, old cottage, located near a wooded area of the farm, which had been used over the years as a starter home for my aunts and uncles.

"This will do me fine," I remember her saying those many years ago as she bravely walked up the steps and into the house. In a strange way, losing her husband and her home all in the space of twenty-four hours made sense to my momma. It was almost as if she had welcomed the burning of her house, as if she knew she could not have lived there without my dad. I had offered a million times to build her a brand-new home with all the modern conveniences, but she would have no part of it.

"Mel," my momma said, opening the screen door. "I was wondering what was taking you so long."

"I was just thinking. I'll be right in."

"No," she murmured, stepping onto the porch. "It's a nice night. Let's sit out here and talk." I helped her over to her rocking chair and lifted her bible from the seat.

My momma's rocking chair was like a queen's throne. My dad may have been the leader of the community, but it was Momma who ruled the family. Her decisions were the final word, and no one questioned her wisdom. She was truly wise.

"So, child, tell me," she asked, "what were you thinking about just now?"

"Oh, I was thinking about the night Pa died," I answered, "and about this old place. Momma, you ought to let me build you a new house. It doesn't have to be fancy or anything, but it should be nice. The old stove, that tiny kitchen—you deserve better than that." I stamped on a loose board in the floor of the porch. "This whole place needs fixin'." I sat down on a porch step.

"You know why I stay here, child?" she asked, reaching over to me. "I stay here to remind my children where they came from. If I lived in some new house, it wouldn't be home to you. Would you stand on the front porch of that new house and remember your daddy the way you did a few minutes ago? Besides, this old rockin' chair is comfortable where it's at. It wouldn't look right anywhere but here. This place keeps our memories alive, and those memories are far too important to be givin' away for the comfort of worldly goods."

"How did you get so smart?" I said, getting up and moving toward her.

"After eighty-six years, you tend to learn a thing or two." She stopped rocking as I laid my head on her lap and felt her fingers caress my cheek. As a child, when I needed her to comfort me, she would stroke my face just as she was doing now.

"What's bothering you, child?" she asked.

"Nothing, Momma," I lied. "Things couldn't be better."

"Now don't you be lyin' to me, you hear? I know when my baby's in trouble. What kind of momma would I be if I didn't know such things? Look at yourself. Tired, sick. The Lord's tryin' to tell you to slow down."

"You know, Momma, the Lord may be telling me to slow down, but in His next breath, He's telling me to get moving. Actually, right about now, I'm not sure if I'm coming or going." I felt very tired, as if the warm Georgia air were coaxing me to sleep. I struggled to keep my eyes open.

"Fightin' the Lord's battle can get confusing at times, but you can't let your enemies see that, sugar. You've got to stand strong."

"What battle are you talkin' about, Momma?" I asked. "What have you heard?" I lifted my head from her lap and saw that she was crying. I knew that missing me wasn't the whole reason behind my momma's tears.

"I know about the reporter," she said, rocking in her chair. "I've seen him snooping around the farm. I may be old, but Son, I don't miss much where my family's concerned."

"So what do you think is going on?" I wasn't sure how much she really knew and how much she was guessing at.

"I feel someone is out to destroy my baby boy," she said, looking into the darkness. "A mother can feel these things. And I know the person that calls me on the phone, saying terrible things about my boy, is an agent of Satan."

"Momma, who's been callin' you?"

"I don't know him by name."

"Oh, Momma," I said, putting my hand to my fore-

179

head. "Was that why you wouldn't answer the phone? Because someone has been asking questions about me?"

"Yes, child, I know that your daddy and I raised up a fine son, and I won't have any part of answering some stranger's questions. 'The wicked lie in wait for the righteous, seeking their very lives; but the Lord will not leave them in their power or let them be condemned when brought to trial.' Tell me, where is its place in the good book?"

"I can't remember right now, Momma," I said.

"Psalm 37:32 and 33," she said. "You'd best remember that."

"I will," I promised. Suddenly, I was hungry.

After eating as much as a sick man could, I went to bed and fell asleep without a problem. No dreams. Just sleep. I didn't get up until noon.

I walked into the kitchen and saw Momma wrapping the food she had cooked and putting it into a large, brown paper bag.

"What are you doing?" I asked.

"Oh, I didn't hear you get up," she said, placing some chicken into the bag. "I'm packin' you some food for your trip home."

"I'm not leaving for a couple of days yet."

"Honey, Norris called about an hour ago. I think you should phone him."

What now? I dialed the youth home's number, but no one answered. I thought I had misdialed and tried again. Still no answer. I called Norris's private line.

"Am I glad you called! We've got big trouble here, Dad. The Pittsburgh newspaper ran a story in today's paper about your troubles with the Legal Aid Society and CYS.

"They've really hit you hard this time. They brought up the gun incident, the problems we had two years ago with our zoning permit, the stolen car, and Richard. What all this has to do with the hearing is beyond me. And they didn't stop there. They interviewed our wonderful neighbor who accused you of shooting at him."

"I shot at him?" I said, hardly believing what Norris was saying. "I think he got his story a little twisted."

"That's not the worst of it," Norris said, his voice rising. "The media reported that you couldn't be found for comment. They're making it sound as if you're on the run. I told them you were in Georgia, but somehow that didn't make it into the story."

"I suppose you've been getting a lot of calls. No one's answering the phone at the youth home."

"Well," Norris explained, "I thought it was best not to answer any more questions until you got home. This is one fire that I can't control. Dad, you know what's happening here, don't you?"

"They're trying to lynch me while I'm out of town."

"You got it!"

I hung up the phone and leaned against the wall. I looked over at Momma, busy packing me food. She always seemed to go on about her business, no matter what the problem. That's what I had to do, too.

A major assault had taken place, and I wasn't there to repel the attack. It was a good strategy on their part, whoever "they" were. I had to get back to the home right away to lead the counterattack.

Suddenly I felt terrible: I was comparing the running of the youth home to fighting a war. But what else could I call it? I was standing knee-deep in casualties.

chapter nineteen
All Things Being Equal

The mass of mankind has not been born with saddles on their backs, nor a favored few booted and spurred, ready to ride them legitimately, by the grace of God.

Thomas Jefferson

A C O L D R A I N was falling when I arrived at the youth home. The white blanket of snow that had covered the ground when I left was almost gone. The colors of the countryside were now dull browns, blacks, and grays. All in all, it was a pretty depressing sight.

I went straight to the administration building to get Carol's assessment of the situation. She had been waiting for me.

"I'm making some hot chocolate," she said, pouring milk into a saucepan. "Do you want some?"

"That sounds real good," I said, removing a mug from the cabinet.

"Well, that will be the last good thing you hear out of me today," Carol said, adding cocoa and sugar to the milk. She stirred the mixture for a couple of minutes, poured us each a cup, then tossed in a few marshmallows.

"Let's hear it," I said, taking a sip.

"I can tell you what's going on in one word: *racism,*

Carol said, pointing her finger at me. "Racism," she repeated.

I hated that word. It made the chocolate in my mouth taste bitter. I had heard the charge of "racism" used too often as an excuse for not taking responsibility. "Well, I certainly can't blame all of our problems on racism," I said, "but I'll . . ."

"Mel, you better start opening your eyes to the forces against you," Carol interrupted, still pointing her finger. "I'm not saying that getting in trouble for hiring a bad counselor, or being understaffed, or spanking a boy is racism. I'm talking about the motivation behind taking you to court instead of talking over the problems and helping you solve them. I'm talking about the motivation behind releasing this story to the press, days after it happened. I'm talking about this article," she said, slamming a newspaper down on the table.

"It's not the Klan and some theatrical cross-burning that's going to force you out," Carol continued. "It's going to be reporting like this, combined with pressure from CYS. You can bet on that."

"You know, Carol," I said, "when I started this place, the only thing I had to guide me was the work that Clint and I had done in Georgia. That program and this one are so different. The people we have to deal with up here are more concerned about paperwork than they are about the kids. But you know something? I don't think anyone else that works with kids in this state has had the problems we've had. And I'm darn sure that if they're doing their job, they're running into the same problems we are. So why us and not them?"

"Because you're a black man who's making a difference," Carol answered, taking a deep breath. "You know me, Mel. I'm not the kind of person who goes around complaining about the color of my skin or using color as a 'poor, poor disadvantaged me' song. I'm not a trouble-maker, I'm not a rebel, but right now, I feel like joining forces with Spike Lee. And the first person I would go after is the reporter who wrote this story, then the editor who allowed it to be printed."

"I don't know how I'm going to handle this yet, but I'll have a decision for you soon."

I finished my hot chocolate and walked over to the classroom in Cabin One to check on the boys. They were so busy reading that they didn't even notice that I had entered the room. I was motioning to the instructor to meet with me when Tony saw me.

"Mr. Mel!" he cried, getting up from his desk and running toward me. The rest of the boys followed. "I was on television."

"So was I," several other boys chimed in.

"Well, I bet you all were a handsome sight to see," I said. "Next thing you know, Hollywood will be after you to do a movie."

"Mr. Mel," Tony said jokingly, "we're good lookin', but we ain't no actors."

"I'm not so sure about that," I said. "I've seen some mighty good performances from you guys on occasion. So what did you think about being on television?"

"Well, they asked me the same questions that guy asked me. I told 'em you never beat me with a strap."

"Listen up, fellahs," I said, walking to the front of the classroom. "I want you all to take your seats. I have something important I want to talk to you about."

They all scrambled to their seats, knocking a few books from the desks in the process, before quietly settling down. I looked around the room at the boys. Something was strange.

"Mr. Walt," I asked the instructor, "are all the boys here?"

"That's all of them," he answered. I knew from the tone in his voice that there was something I hadn't been told yet, something that was very, very wrong. Then it struck me. All the white boys in the program were gone.

"Mr. Walt, can we talk in private?" I asked, motioning toward the bathroom.

"Sure thing, Mr. Mel," he answered.

"I'll be right back," I told the boys. "In the meantime, you guys get back to work, and I better not hear a sound from you. Henry, you're the class monitor."

Mr. Walt entered the bathroom, and I closed the door after him. "What's going on?"

"CYS came by early this morning and removed all the white kids from the program," he answered. "They said it had nothing to do with the accusations and all. It's just that they found places for them to live."

"They found 'places'? Are you kidding me?"

"Hey, I'm only telling you what they said," Walt explained, shrugging his shoulders. "I'm not asking you to believe them."

"Well, I don't," I said, glimpsing my reflection in the bathroom mirror. The anger I saw in my eyes frightened even me. *Calm yourself. Calm yourself. You can't let the boys see you like this.* I turned to Walt and began unloading on him.

"So, if I'm understanding the situation correctly, here you have a black man," I said, slapping myself on the chest, "who starts a youth home so he can beat little boys. And it's okay to beat them, as long as they're little black boys. The next thing you know, they'll be accusing me of racism for not having white kids in the program. Am I crazy for seeing things this way?"

"Nope," said Walt, "I don't think you're crazy, Mel. In fact, I think you'd be off your rocker if you didn't see it that way. Question is, what are you going to do about it? Worse yet, what can be done?"

I didn't know. I couldn't allow myself to react when I was angry, and at that moment I was very angry.

"I'm going out there to have a talk with the boys," I said, turning on the water faucet. I splashed some water on my face and struggled to regain my composure. I didn't like the thought of involving the boys in this ridiculous war, but they needed to hear straight from me the problems that faced us. After all, this was their home, and, at the moment, I was their only family.

185

    I left the bathroom and stood before the boys. "Guys," I began, "Mr. Walt says you're all doing well in your studies. I want you to know I'm proud of you, and I want to thank you for working so hard.

    "Now I have something else to tell you that's very important. Recently, some people have been saying bad things about me. They've accused me of hurting you boys. You and I know the truth, but sometimes knowing the truth isn't enough. Sometimes you have to go out and fight for the truth, and that's what I'm going to do. I don't expect that it's going to be easy. The bad things they're saying about me are probably going to get worse before they get better.

    "Your caseworkers are going to ask you to report anything you don't like about this place. They're going to ask you lots of questions about the counselors and me, and you must tell them the truth. That's the way to fight for what is right. You always tell the truth. Don't let them twist your words around or get you to say something that you know didn't happen. If anyone tells you to lie, you let me know.

    "I want you all to remember, no matter what happens, that I care for you. Sometimes I know you don't understand why I put you on restrictions or why I holler at you, but everything I do is because I want you boys to grow up to be fine young men. I want you to finish school, go to college, and learn that anything is possible through hard work and discipline. Boys, in this world, there's no such thing as luck.

    "Just one more thing. If any of you don't trust me, I want you to tell Mr. Walt, Mr. Pete, or any of the other counselors by the end of the day. We'll sit down together and see if we can't work out our differences. Does anyone have something they'd like to say?"

    "Mr. Mel," Tony said, rising from his chair. "I heard Miss Susan say that the judge is gonna throw you in jail for helpin' black kids. If they do that to you, the guys and me want you to know that we'll come break you out. I know you're gonna say that it's against the law, Mr. Mel, but we've already decided. We can run away and start another youth home somewhere else."

The boys always found a way to lighten up my spirits with their innocence. I couldn't hold back my laughter as I pictured them dressed as little cowboys, hopping mad, shooting play pistols.

"Nobody's putting me in jail," I assured them. "But thanks for being so concerned."

I said good-bye to the boys and headed to Norris's office. He handed me a stack of newspapers as I walked through the door. "You better sit down and read these so we can plan how to handle this."

I read through the articles: "Blount unaware of youth home allegations. Yesterday neighbor registers another complaint, says Blount fired a shot that hit only yards away from where neighbor was cutting grass. Boys sent to horse trailer or stall to calm down. Children may have been subjected to ridicule or humiliation. Youth home under-staffed. No staff therapist. No staff nutritionist. Program seriously flawed. Major deficiencies plague youth home. Home source of controversy. Suit alleges beatings at Blount home."

"You know what the sad thing is about all this?" I said. Norris looked up at me. "Once people read something in the paper, they believe it. It doesn't matter what's true and what isn't."

"You're probably right," Norris replied, "but that doesn't mean you have to sit back and take it. Your reputation's on the line here."

"Do you think that I don't know that? But I can't get sidetracked. I don't want to be turned into a spokesman for black rights. I want to run a youth home. If I can just get some kids through the program, get their lives turned around, that will show the black and white communities that we can make a difference. We've got to show them, because telling them just doesn't work anymore. They've heard it all before. Of course, I sympathize with all minorities. Hey, I was brought up in a time far worse than this one. I fought back. I fought back by being the best. Do you understand what I'm saying?"

"Yes, I do." Norris walked over, picked up some file folders and handed them to me. "But when they pulled all the white kids out of here, I knew you had to show them that we wouldn't stand for this sort of treatment, this slap in the face. You let them get away with this and you might as well kiss the program good-bye." He tapped the folders in my hand. "These are the white kids' files. Take a look. Not one of them was ready to be released from the program."

I didn't have to look at the files. I knew what was going on. I had seen it often and had almost fallen victim to it. Racism. There was no escape from it, and no law could kill it. There would be no relief from its ugliness until people ceased being afraid.

"I'm being drawn into a bad situation," I said, laying the folders on Norris's desk. "I don't want to go before the media and even mention the word 'racism,' because if I do, I know they're going to say the only reason I think there are charges against me is because I'm black. They won't hear what I'm really saying because they won't understand what I'm talking about. They've never experienced being black in a white world. That's another thing. Doesn't this town have any black reporters?"

"Let's not open that can of worms now." The phone rang and Norris answered it. "It's Annie."

"What are you going to do?" She always got right to the point.

"Well. . . ."

"You know what I'd do?" Annie asked, not giving me time to answer. "I'd take the newspaper on. Listen, for the most part, I'm very naive. I've never been personally involved in race issues, and frankly, I don't like knowing that I am. As stupid as this may sound, I see people, not color.

"I can only guess that being black in an all-white world is like being a woman in an all-male world. And it isn't pretty. That being the case, you'd better start screaming 'racism' real loud. Maybe somebody will hear you."

"Well, I've screamed it before and it didn't get me too far," I said.

"Consider doing it again. I know you're busy, but I want you to read an article in this evening's paper. It's about a white man who beat his eleven-month-old baby to death because his form of 'discipline' got out of hand. The courts gave him five months' probation. There's something really wrong here. Now I'll let you get back to your thinking. And, Mel . . ."

"Yes, Annie?"

"I'll say a prayer for you. But I'm just not sure that God hears me anymore. On second thought, you better talk to Him yourself."

One of these days, I promised myself, I'm gonna have a talk with that girl about her relationship with God. She always seemed to be dropping hints that they were on shaky ground, but now was not the time for a discussion about religion.

I hung up the phone. I felt the rope tightening around my neck. I either had to fight back with the only weapon I had available to me—to call for a press conference and accuse the media and the system of racism—or be strangled to death. I didn't think the Lord wanted me showing up on His doorstep just yet, but I knew racism well enough to understand one thing: You can feel it and be affected by it, but you can't always make other people see it.

"Norris," I said, "set up a press conference. Looks like I have to do battle."

I went home, sat in front of the fireplace, and waited for TiAnda to come home. The warmth of the fire felt good, and I could feel myself beginning to relax. I thought about my momma. My visit with her seemed like a hundred years ago. I smiled when I thought of her cooking all that food. That reminded me: It was still sitting in the trunk of my car. Maybe Momma wasn't that far away after all.

chapter twenty

The Press Conference

Sufficient to each day are the duties to be done and the trials to be endured. God never built a Christian strong enough to carry today's duties and tomorrow's anxieties piled on top of them.

Theodore Russell Lowell

I S L E P T surprisingly easy for a man who was about to face a firing squad. One dream, however, remained with me. I was standing on my mountaintop, looking over the town. It was summer, and the fields were rich with golden wheat. Wind grazed nearby in a green pasture. A sudden breeze swept the Stetson from my head, and I watched as it tumbled down the hillside and disappeared into a cave. Suddenly, my dad was standing beside me, holding my hat in his hands. "Hi, Pa," I said, not at all surprised to see him. "Sure is a pretty day."

The mountain faded away. My dad and I were sitting under a big oak tree. I could see children playing in the distance, but I didn't recognize them. I wondered who they all belonged to and why there were so many of them.

A dead groundhog dangled from a rope above me. Tiny droplets of blood fell upon my head and ran down my forehead and into my eyes. I kept wiping at the blood with my hand, but the more I wiped it away, the more it kept coming. Strangely, I wasn't upset. I just kept talking to my dad as I tried to clear the blood from my eyes.

Then my dad stood up and placed the Stetson on my head. The blood stopped. The groundhog fell from the tree and ran into a hole. And I woke up.

I sat on the edge of my bed, thinking that the dream had the makings of a nightmare, although somehow it wasn't frightening. It didn't leave me with an eerie feeling that made me want to shudder. Instead, I felt renewed. I read somewhere that dreams take place because the subconscious is working out our problems while we sleep. Dreams are supposed to be a safety valve that keeps us sane.

Regardless of what dreams are or what purpose they serve, I knew this dream had given me faith. All those children belonged to no one. They were discards, searching for a home. I knew that the blood of fear would someday be washed away by the love of the Father. I had to believe that.

Before the press conference, TiAnda, Norris, Denitia, and I prayed together. I asked the Lord to guide my words and not allow me to stumble. Please, I prayed, raise me up from the lion's den so that I may continue to serve You. Save me from words of anger, deceit and despair.

I was ready. With TiAnda by my side, I walked into the room where the press was waiting. I wasn't a stranger to the media, but I felt like a rookie when I saw so many cameras aimed at me, microphones being thrust in my direction, and all those reporters. Then I saw my boys standing in the corner of the room.

"Norris, what are they doing here?" I asked, pointing to the boys. "I don't think they should be here."

"Well, they took a vote. They think you need them, and so do I. Let them stay, Dad. Besides, they should see you fighting for them."

I motioned for the boys to join me at the front of the room. Everyone fell silent as twelve little boys made their way to me. "I'm glad you all could make it," I said.

"We're here for you, Mr. Mel," Henry said. "We won't let them hurt you." At that moment, I would have swum

191

the Atlantic, climbed Mount Everest, or walked across Death Valley for my boys.

Instead, I stood still, waiting for God's power to strike me like a lightning bolt and turn my tongue into the smooth, swift sword of truth. I waited to be possessed by God's righteousness and strength so that my words would be divine. But there was no lightning bolt or possession. There was only me, a humble servant doing the best he humanly could.

"If you look back through American history, you will see that evil people have burned, lynched, and drowned those they have feared. And do you know what things evil people fear most? Goodness, kindness, understanding, and love. Those evil people were determined to destroy the foundation of freedom that this nation was built on, but they didn't succeed. The burnings and drownings have stopped, but not the lynchings. They just got a lot more sophisticated. We have entered an age of high-tech lynching. We no longer have to use a rope. We can use the media, the government, the court system. Heck, the lynchee doesn't even have to be present. He could be, say, visiting his momma in Georgia when someone decides to hang him.

"But ladies and gentleman, obviously the rope broke, because here I am, standing before you. I'm not running and I'm not hiding, because I know what Mel Blount is and isn't about. Mel Blount isn't about hurting kids. And he isn't about lying. He will not allow you or anyone else to lynch him.

"I'm a black man doing something that's not usual for a black person to do. I've set up shop where there are no blacks, and I'm succeeding. My work challenges the racist notion that black children should live unproductive lives on the street so they can grow up to be unproductive adults living on the street.

"This whole thing is not about child abuse, because the CYS and the Legal Aid Society know they can't prove their accusations. Their accusations are only part of a systematic approach to destroy this program, and my character assassination is part of their plan.

"Now I'm sure the people from the CYS and the Legal Aid Society are going to tell you just what they told me, that they're only reacting to what their clients have told them about the goings-on at the home. They'll tell you it's their job to protect their clients.

"First of all, their clients are our children. Secondly, what they are protecting is their own jobs. The Mel Blount Youth Home does not believe in giving lip service about helping children. We actually do it. It doesn't matter if that child is white, black, red, yellow or has rainbow stripes. But it's obvious that color makes a difference to the CYS. Look at my boys. Do you see any white kids among them? Doesn't it make you wonder why?

"The only person that is being abused here is me, and I'm not going to allow you or anybody else to use me as a whipping post. I can't allow you to break me, because if I break, so does this program.

"These kids love me because I stand for something. All our boys, unless they're lying to me, say that they love living at the youth home. I challenge any one of you to find a single piece of evidence that proves these kids have been hurt. I've admitted to spanking one of the boys. That spanking was the last resort. There's a big difference between child abuse and discipline. I feel very good about everything we've done here. I know my staff is working hard. I know they're caring people. I know we're doing good things.

"I'm hard-pressed to see the difference between the doings of the Ku Klux Klan and the child advocacy groups. Both are destructive and self-serving. The CYS and the Legal Aid Society will tell you that my program has not been singled out. When's the last time some other youth facility made front-page news? When's the last time you've heard of any youth facility's undergoing the scrutiny that we have endured? When's the last time CYS or the Legal Aid Society called the media to give them negative information on a child care facility? That's where you in the media are getting your tips, aren't you? Well, I can guarantee they'll be giving you more information about the youth home. And I can guarantee you that, no matter what the CYS and Legal Aid Society do or say, we will endure. Now that I've said my piece, you go on and ask me any questions you'd like."

"Mr. Blount," one reporter asked, "are you saying that CYS and the Klan are working together?"

"No. I'm saying that I just don't see much difference between the two."

"The CYS reported that you humiliated the boys. They said that some of your procedures show a total lack of understanding of what is involved in caring for youth. Those procedures include making the kids wear brightly colored pants that identify them as potential runners; using the horse trailer as a time-out room, and getting the boys out of bed at five-thirty every morning. How do you respond to that?"

"If my boys were embarrassed because they were caught doing something they shouldn't, well, chances are they should have been embarrassed. Are the counselors and I sometimes tough with the boys? Yes, we are. Do we ridicule them? No. Do we get upset and sometimes say things we shouldn't? Yes. Did I make some boys wear pants that were different from the other boys' pants? Yes.

"The CYS told me that I was making the runners feel different. Well, they were different. They had a history of running away. Check their charts. If we had three boys wearing 'runners' pants' and only two were present, the counselors knew right away to start looking. Besides, the boys who were runners had to come to grips with the fact that they were different from the rest of the boys and that we intended to keep a close eye on them until their behavior changed. They had to earn the right to dress the same as the other boys. I don't see how that's humiliating. But CYS said to stop it, so we did."

The questions went on and on. Finally the session broke up, and only one reporter was left. We walked to the door together. "You're not going to win this battle, Mr. Blount," he said, with a little too much emotion.

"What makes you say that?" I asked. I had seen this man before, but I couldn't place where. His eyes looked very familiar. Suddenly, I knew I was standing face-to-face with "the stranger."

"Because you're not wanted here."

"Well, son, maybe so. But I'm not out to win the battle. I'm out to win the war."

He laughed. "Mr. Blount," he said, changing his tone completely, "I wish you the best. I honestly do. You're doing a great thing here." It was no surprise to me that the warmth in his words of goodwill was not reflected in his eyes.

I stopped and watched him walk out the door. "Sam," I called to him.

"Yes?" he said, turning around.

"Don't you be calling my momma anymore, you hear?"

"I don't know what you're talking about," he answered and hurried away.

After the press conference, the staff, the boys, and I returned to our chores. There was a lot of work for me to catch up on, so I had little time to think about what I had said to the press. I had done what I felt was right. I had thrown a stone into the pond, and I expected ripples.

chapter twenty-one
The Rebellion

As long as our social order regards the good of institutions rather than the good of men, so long will there be a vocation for the rebel.

Richard Roberts

I D I D M Y S E L F a favor and didn't read the newspaper reports on the press conference. Hearing about them from TiAnda, Norris, Carol, and Annie were enough for me.

"Boy, am I glad I'm not married to this man," TiAnda said teasingly as she looked up from the newspaper.

"Who?" I asked, playing right into her hands.

"This dumb, old ex-football player who's all force and no compassion, muscles and no smarts, who has goals but no vision."

"Who'd he play for?" I asked, reaching for the paper.

"The Steelers."

"What's his name?"

"I'll give you a clue," TiAnda said, keeping the newspaper from me. "He's in the Hall of Fame. He went to four Super Bowls. He owns a youth home, and he beats up on little kids. Give up?"

"Get outta here!" I said, catching on to her joke. *One of these days,* I thought to myself, *before I go to meet my maker, I*

*would like someone to recognize me first as a founder of a youth
home and second as an ex-football player. Why do they always find
it necessary to talk about something that happened fifteen, twenty
years ago?*

"You were one bad football player," TiAnda commented, as she quoted some statistics from the newspaper, "and
that's why articles on you always start or end with your
football career. You were one of the best because you played
harder, and the paper wants to remind the reader of that,
because if you played football harder than most, it's easy to
believe that you're capable of being just as tough and
ruthless with children. They're trying to make you look like
the stereotype of a football player, you know . . . all strength
and no brains. And it looks like they succeeded, and not
only in what they wrote."

She showed me the picture that accompanied the story.
It was terrible. I looked fierce and intimidating, as if I were
ready to take on the Cleveland Browns all by myself. "Do
you think people really see me this way?"

"Well, I know I don't," TiAnda answered.

"Does that mean everyone else does?"

TiAnda sighed and fell silent. She finished reading the
paper while I called the courthouse to find out if Richard's
hearing was still on for that morning. It was. I had promised
him that I would be there. The judge would allow me to say
a few words on Richard's behalf, but I wasn't expecting that
I would do much good.

I stopped by the office to get Richard's file and found
Carol already busy taking phone calls about new articles on
the youth home. "Contributors are dropping like flies,"
Carol whispered, covering the mouthpiece of the phone
with her hand.

I expected it. I knew that the NFL had some work
planned for me and that would help us out for a little while.
Maybe I could get a few more speeches squeezed in
somewhere. I had pulled the home out of some tight spots
before, and I was sure that I could do it again. Money! I truly
do detest it, in a way.

When I arrived at the courthouse, Richard was talking with his social worker. Although I couldn't hear their words, I could see that the conversation was so upsetting to Richard that he started to pound his fist on the table. I hadn't seen him do that in a long time. Then I remembered the manger and how proud Richard had been when he put it together. Pretty soon we'd be taking the manger out of storage and setting it up again. Only this time, Richard wouldn't be there to supervise.

The judge walked in and didn't waste any time getting down to business. It was over and done with, just that quick. I pleaded with the judge to allow me to have custody, but I was denied. Richard was sentenced to Grandville until he turned eighteen.

"Don't forget about me, Mr. Mel," he said as they took him away. He seemed quiet and resigned, but I'll never forget the look of fear in his eyes.

Maybe it was because I was tired and not feeling so good, or maybe it was because I loved that boy, but my emotions got the better of me. I had to go into the men's room to pull myself together.

When I got back to the youth home, I told the boys what had happened to Richard. They were upset but not surprised. "This happens all the time," Tony said. "The streets ain't no place for kids. I'm never leavin' here, Mr. Mel, 'cause if I do, the same thing will happen to me." Unfortunately, Tony would be turning fourteen in a couple of months.

I visited with the counselors, the cook, the cleaning lady. Everyone's morale seemed to take a nosedive. Some of the counselors confided in me that they felt unsure about how to handle the boys. They felt intimidated by the accusations of the CYS and the media, especially the Pittsburgh newspaper. They were suspicious about the Department of Public Welfare officials who had arrived that morning to begin their investigation into the allegations of the CYS. It seemed to me that they should have investigated me first, then taken me to court.

I promised myself that I would keep up with my paperwork. If the state and county wanted me to do everything in triplicate, I'd have to learn to live with it.

I was busy looking through some files in a room adjoining the dining hall when I heard the boys entering for their meal. They were a little noisier than usual. I was surprised that the counselors were allowing the shouting matches I heard between several of the boys. After a few minutes, when they still hadn't calmed down, I decided to see what was going on. I stood in the hall unnoticed and watched as they began moving toward the food.

"Okay, guys, get in line and help yourselves," one of the counselors said, taking the lids off the various pots and pans that were on the serving table.

"No, wait a minute," I said, stepping into their view. "There isn't going to be any food put on this table tonight until you boys stop talking. So what will it be, food or talk?"

The boys stopped talking. I nodded to the counselors to resume serving dinner and left the room. I stood in the hall just in case my message wasn't clear to all of the boys. And it wasn't. The loud talk erupted among them again. I walked back into the room.

"That's it, fellahs," I said. "Get over to your chairs and sit down. Now! I don't want to hear a word out of any of you. It doesn't matter to me if you eat a hot meal now or a cold meal later. That's your choice. But I think I'll have mine hot."

I walked over, grabbed a plate and served myself some food. I sat down near the boys and began eating. "Hot or cold? Which is it?"

"Hot," they answered quietly.

"Okay, then line up." As they helped themselves to beef stew, biscuits, and salad, all I could hear was the clinking of a few dishes. I waited until they were all seated, then picked up my plate and headed back to the office.

"What a jerk," I heard one of the boys whisper as soon as I had turned my back. The voice was familiar. I knew the offender.

Without turning around, I said, "Kyle, you're on restriction for a month. You'll eat your meals alone until I say you can join the rest of the boys, and you'll have all the stalls cleaned before breakfast. And one more thing. After you finish eating, I want to talk to you."

He didn't protest then. But once in the privacy of my office, Kyle proceeded to threaten me.

"I don't have to clean no stalls," he said, putting his feet on my desk. "You must think we're all your personal slaves. Well, I ain't nobody's slave."

"Are you finished, or is there something else you'd like to say?" I asked. "Because if that's all you have to say for yourself, you're on restriction for two months, you'll eat your meals with me, and you'll clean the stalls every morning for the next week. Now is there anything else you'd care to add?"

"You think you can scare me, don't you?" he said, leaning back on his chair until he was balancing it on two legs. "Well, I've got one on you, Mel. I'm gonna tell the newspaper on you, and if you think you have trouble now . . . well, you ain't even begun to know what trouble is. I just may tell a story or two to those investigators. What do you think of that?"

All sons challenge their fathers. I remembered the day I challenged mine. First came the whuppin', then came the talkin'.

The difference between my dad and me and Kyle and me was that Kyle believed that he held all the cards. Lying and hurting had been a way of life for him, and, of course, I wasn't really his father. But the fact remained that Kyle was still a child who needed adult guidance and supervision.

"You know, Kyle, the more you talk, the deeper you dig yourself into a hole," I said, removing his feet from my desk. "First, you got yourself into trouble for cursing. Then you got in more trouble for cursing and mouthing off. Now you're in serious trouble for threatening to tell a lie. I'll tell you what. You go to the newspaper and the investigators and you tell your lies, but that isn't going to get you out of the barn any sooner."

"What are you going to do, force me?" he asked, putting his feet back on the desk. "You gonna get up each morning, get me dressed and drag me down to the barn?"

"I'll even put the shovel in your hand," I said, sitting back in my chair. "Kyle, we can sit here all night threatening each other, but that won't accomplish anything. Do you know why I'm so strict with you?"

"I know what you're gonna say, 'cause you care,'" Kyle said sarcastically.

"Do you believe that's true?" I asked. He didn't answer right away.

"Yeah, I suppose you do," he said, removing his feet from the desk. "It's just that I don't like anyone telling me what to do."

"Kyle, I think it's more than that," I said. "I think you're trying to take the easy way out. You see that we're having some problems around here, and you think you can take advantage of those problems. What you really should be doing right now is fightin' for this place.

"Doing the right thing is almost always harder, but in the end, the rewards are greater. Look at Richard. It was harder for him to stay out of trouble than it was to get into it. And where's Richard now? Locked up. I didn't want that to happen to him, and I won't let it happen to you.

"Kyle, I need your help. I'm going through a bad time here. I'm fighting to keep these doors open. I'm asking you to be strong. Set a good example for the rest of the boys. You know, you are the oldest." Kyle thought about it for a little while. "Okay, Mr. Mel. I'll try, but I'm not promising anything."

"Good enough," I said.

"Do I still have to clean the stalls?"

"Commit the crime, pay the fine."

"Does that mean 'yes'?" he asked, standing up.

I looked at him and nodded.

"I thought so," he said, walking out the door.

· · ·

It was Kyle's last day of barn duty, and I was talking with him while he was laying down fresh straw in the horse stalls when Annie arrived unexpectedly. I hadn't seen or heard much from her since Richard was sentenced.

"It's a little early for class, isn't it?" I asked, as she walked into the barn bundled from head to foot as if she were about to set off on an Antarctic expedition.

"This is too early even for the birds," Annie said, "but I want to talk to you, and I figured that the only way that would happen is if I got here before sunrise. Seems like you're always in a meeting or away giving a speech or something."

"Tell me about it," I answered.

"Can we get out of this cold?" Annie asked, pulling her coat tight about her shoulders. "I really belong on Maui, you know, or maybe the Riviera. Somewhere warm."

"Didn't you grow up around here?" I asked.

"Yep," she answered, as we walked across the road. "But I think my parents stole me away from some tropical island and I've been a prisoner here in Pennsylvania ever since. But I didn't come here to talk about that."

"Oh?" I said, opening the door to the farmhouse. Annie walked over to the fireplace and began rubbing her hands together. "Is anything wrong?"

"Mel, did you hear what happened in class last week?"

"No."

"The boys were behaving pretty well, considering everything that's taken place lately. Anyway, I decided to divide the boys into groups—you know, the editing staff, the writers, the artists. Then, for no apparent reason, Alton rips his shirt off, grabs a chair, and threatens to bust Henry over the head with it."

"We've been having lots of problems with Alton lately. In fact, we've been having problems with most of the boys. What did you do?"

"At first, I didn't know what to do. I never had this happen with any of the boys before. I tried to talk with him and get him to calm down so I didn't have to call a counselor. I thought I had him under control because he put down the chair, but then he began strutting back and forth across the room, flexing his muscles. He backed me into a corner and made a few suggestive remarks. That's when Kyle came to my aid. The counselors must have heard the commotion, because they came running into the room and finally talked Alton into leaving the room with them.

"But that's not the only problem. Since Alton lost control, I've asked one of the counselors to always be in the room with me during class. Well, one of the boys smacked the counselor twice in the head, 'accidentally,' and challenged the counselor to hit him back so he could 'tell' the newspaper. That same evening, another boy kept jabbing his pencil into the seat of his chair, puncturing the vinyl covering. The best the counselor could do was threaten to tell you."

Annie's experiences were nothing new to me. I was hearing the same kind of horror stories from most of the volunteers. I couldn't be around all the time, especially since we were nearing the holidays, my best time for fundraising. Besides, CYS and the Legal Aid Society had made it clear that I was not allowed to have anything to do with disciplining the boys until after the investigation. But if they didn't hurry and finish their work, the inmates would soon be in control of the prison, so to speak.

"Annie," I explained, "my hands are all but tied."

"Then you're going to have to find a new, more inventive way to influence the boys. They're falling apart, and they need you more than ever."

Annie was right. "Any suggestions?" Stupid question. She always had suggestions.

"Yeah," she said, seating herself next to the fire. "If you can't take part in disciplining the boys, then get more involved in other activities with them. Plan more field trips, hold some group talks, be a part of our Thursday night class. Go blaze some more trails with the boys. Show them more chipmunks."

"I don't know, I'm squeezed for time as it is, Annie.

We're running out of money fast and I've been hustling to keep something in the coffers. But I'll find the time for your suggestions somehow."

"One other thing, Mel," she said, "You might try opening up to the kids more. Tell them stories about when you were growing up. Let them hear about some of the troubles you got yourself into when you were their age. Read them stories. You read the Bible every day, don't you? Well, read it to them. You're always quoting from Proverbs to me, for some reason. Why not quote some verses to the boys and explain how the Bible relates to their everyday life?"

That sounded like a hint to me, maybe even a call for help. The time was right for the question I'd wanted to ask her before. "Can I ask you something personal?"

"Sure."

"Do you believe in Christ?"

She smiled. "What does that have to do with anything?"

"Just curious."

Annie didn't say anything for a while. She just stared at the fire. She must have finally begun to warm up because she unbuttoned her coat. "You want to know the truth? I'm just not sure what I believe in anymore. I was raised Catholic, but now I don't know what I am. Maybe Jesus and I had a falling out."

"Sometimes a child has to rebel against her parents," I said. "Sooner or later, though, that child finds her way back home."

"Well, speaking of home," Annie said, buttoning up her coat, "that's where I better start heading."

"No, don't go yet," I said, moving toward her. "Let's talk about this." Annie gave me a sideways glance, and I could tell that she was feeling mighty uncomfortable. "I just want to help you, that's all," I said, feeling that it was important that she talk about her loss of faith. "You're a very generous and giving person. You don't seem. . . ."

"What? Unchristian-like?" I clearly heard the sarcasm in her voice.

"Annie, come on, ease up. You and me, we trust one another."

She sighed deeply. "You're right, Mel, I do trust you. It's hard for me to talk about this. I don't remember exactly when or why I started to question my religion. But when I realized I was having doubts, I asked the Lord to give me a reason to believe in Him and His son. I don't remember ever getting an answer, just pain and suffering, around me and inside me.

"Don't get me wrong, I want to believe. Believing would make my life much easier. I've looked hard to find something to believe in. I can't begin to tell you how many alternative forms of worship I've looked into. I've even worn a crystal necklace, hoping it would raise my consciousness.

"Now I know in my heart I want to go home to God and Jesus, but I don't know how to reach them. I want to believe they are guiding my steps down a path that is especially meant for me to travel. If I only knew that for sure, I wouldn't care if I had to crawl the whole way."

"Annie, we're having a prayer meeting tonight, what do you say you crawl on over here and join us?"

"Well . . . yes, okay," she replied, apparently surprised at her own answer. "I'm not sure why, but I'll be there."

After Annie left, I joined Kyle for breakfast. We were still having our meals together. As we were eating, Norris walked into the office with a big smile on his face. "Guess what?"

"What?" I said, with a mouth full of food.

"Go on and guess." Norris insisted. "What's the best thing that could happen right now?"

"Norris. . . ."

"All right," he said, handing me the newspaper. "The Scaife Family Foundation is going to give us $150,000 for our building program. And look what they said about us in the newspaper. The trustees don't believe the allegations, and they're behind us one hundred percent. Is this great or what?"

I felt like standing up and shouting "Hallelujah." In fact, I did.

"I have some more good news, and I know you'll think I'm making this up." Norris said, smiling like the cat that ate the canary.

"Well, are you going to tell me or do I have to guess?"

"This just came over the fax." He handed me a piece of paper.

It was from the White House. The President was coming to Pittsburgh and wanted to meet me! I had been chosen as his 524th "Point of Light."

What a day this had shaped up to be.

•   •   •

Reverend Johnson joined us for our prayer meeting that evening. Annie showed up a bit late, but I could hardly be irritated with her. This was a big step for her. She didn't say anything, which for Annie was highly unusual. She just listened. Then, before the meeting was over, Annie got up, smiled at me, and walked out the door. I was sure that I saw a tear in her eye. I couldn't tell if it was a tear of joy or sorrow.

chapter twenty-two

The President Extends
a Helping Hand

I feel coming on a strange disease—humility.

Frank Lloyd Wright

I W A S nervous. I was going to meet the President of the United States. Me. The son of a Georgia farmer. I still couldn't believe it. President Bush had decided to honor me by choosing me as one of his daily "Points of Light."

I read the White House memo over and over. The more I read it, the more humble I became. I hadn't felt this way since Cliff Branch outran me and I was benched.

Probably any other time I would have been a little cynical about a member of the government handing out such glittering praise, but when the President of the United States was singling me out for an award, I was suddenly Mr. Patriotism. I've always loved my country, but that has never stopped me from doing my share of complaining, especially where African-Americans and children were concerned. I even spoke before the United States Senate and pleaded with them to help our children.

Despite the problems that face America, especially concerning race relations, traditional values, and ethics, I'm hard pressed to believe any place else is better. The Lord promised us a land of milk and honey, and America, for all its faults, is it.

TiAnda and Alton got into the car with me, and we headed to the airport. Only one boy was allowed to join us, and Alton was chosen because of his excellent behavior during the previous few weeks. Because we were so excited, we couldn't stop talking.

"Mr. Pete says we're VIPs—Very Important People," Alton said, nervously thumping his foot against the back of my seat. "We're gonna have a talk with 'the man' himself."

"Well," I laughed. "I may get to say a word or two, but I don't think you will. And if you do get the opportunity to say something, I don't want you calling him 'the man'. You address him as Mr. President, got it?"

"Yeah, yeah," Alton answered. "I know."

"And another thing. Quit kicking my seat."

"Sorry."

As we drove on, I thought about my dad. If it weren't for him, I would have never left the farm. He knew my planting and harvesting would be of a different kind. Wherever he was, I hoped that I had done him proud.

"This is a day you can tell your grandchildren about," I said. "They'll be very proud of you."

"Gee, Mr. Mel," Alton said. I could see him in the rearview mirror, sticking his tongue out as if he'd just tasted something bitter. "I'm not havin' any kids. I don't need the problems. What if they turn out like me?"

"And what's wrong with you?" I asked, making a left turn into the airport short-term parking lot.

"You don't have the time right now to hear my list of problems," he answered. "Maybe some other time."

"Well, you're right. Things are gonna get pretty hectic for us in a few minutes. But as soon as we get the chance, I'm gonna hear that list of yours."

When we entered the airport building, we were greeted by the secret service. They quickly escorted us to the VIP room, where we were briefed while we waited for the President's plane to land.

When the plane arrived, we were ushered to the landing field. The wind was blowing and there was a light drizzle. My long riding coat flapped in the wind, but my Stetson sat firmly on my head. We waited. Finally, the door of the plane opened.

"Do you think that President Bush would take us for a plane ride if we asked?" Alton whispered, tugging on my coat.

"We're not going to ask," I said firmly, staring down at him, "are we?"

"No, sir," he answered. "It was just a thought."

We waited. Then President Bush appeared. He stood on the platform, waved to the crowd, and descended the stairs. He walked over to me.

"Well, hello, Mr. Blount," he said, shaking my hand. "I hear you are doing a wonderful job with our youth."

"Thank you, Mr. President," I said, "It's an honor for me to be meeting with you today." The President stopped and looked at me. I mean, he *looked* at me.

"Mr. Blount, it's an honor for me to be meeting you," he said. "Now who is this little fellow?"

Alton gave the President a firm handshake then boldly and rather loudly introduced himself. "Hello, Mr. President. My name is Alton." *Good*, I thought, *Alton handled that very well*.

Then Alton continued, "I sure would love to see the inside of your plane."

"You would?" The President laughed. "Well, then, let's see. I think we have time for a short tour."

"Really?" Alton asked, grinning like a Cheshire cat. *Really?* I thought.

"Really." The President said, taking Alton's hand.

We toured the President's plane, and I must admit, I was pretty close to being in shock. After our tour, the President turned to me and said, "Keep making America strong, Mr. Blount."

"I will," I vowed.

Just like that, it was over. President Bush had a meeting to get to and I had a youth home to run.

When we arrived back at the home, Alton couldn't wait to share the details of his visit with the President.

"Mr. Pete," Alton said, smiling from ear to ear. "President Bush said that being chosen as a 'Point of Light' is like being in the Hall of Fame, only not for playing football but for working to make our country a better place to live. He said the youth home was making the country better by making us kids better. Isn't that so, Mr. Mel?"

"Well, yes," I answered. "That's what I'm working at doing."

"So if we become better people when we grow up, we can help make kids like us better. Then we can get indicted into the Point of Light Hall of Fame."

I smiled. "Inducted," I corrected him. "What do you guys say we all go for a walk?" I felt as if I had some extra energy to burn off. "I'll change and meet you in front of the barn."

I hurried to change my clothes, then met up with the boys. They were a sight to see, all bundled up in their winter coats, hats, and gloves. As we headed up the hillside, I asked Alton to walk beside me.

"So," I said, "let's hear that list."

"Aw, Mr. Mel," Alton said, with a wave of his hand. "You know my problems. I got a bad temper, I'm not real book-smart. Miss Annie's doing what she can to teach me to read and write, but I'm the worst one in the class. I pick on kids littler than me."

"Well, I don't think there's anything on that list that we can't work at fixing," I said. "Maybe Miss Annie can come a little early and work with you, one-on-one. You're working with the counselors and the psychologist to understand why you have such a temper, and they're going to help you find a way to get it under control. You know, I used to have a pretty bad temper myself."

"Nah—you?" Alton said, shaking his head.

"Yes," I nodded. "But my dad told me that a bad temper is just a sign of a deep anger we don't understand, and I believe that's true. Heck, half the time I couldn't even tell what I was so angry at. Maybe somebody said or did something that triggered a bad memory. It's hard to tell why one thing makes us angry and another thing doesn't. My dad used to tell me to take that anger and hold it in my hand. He told me to stop and take a real good look at it before I threw it in some other person's direction."

"So what did you do after you looked at it?" Alton asked.

"I prayed."

"What good did that do?" He asked, obviously not liking my answer. "How does praying stop you from wanting to hit someone?"

"First of all, it slows down the anger," I answered, stooping to pick up a stone. "Once the anger is slowed down, you can begin to think a little more clearly." I handed Alton the stone. "Pretend someone called you a bad name and made you angry. That stone is your anger. Now look at it. Do you see the stone or the person that made you angry?"

"I see the stone," he answered.

"Good. That means you're in control of your anger. Remember that the stone is your anger. You can ask it any question you like and it has to answer you. But before you give your anger away, you must listen carefully to its answer. After you talk with your anger, then decide what is best to do with it."

"What did you do with yours?" Alton asked, staring at the stone.

"I gave mine to the Lord," I said.

"And what did He do with it?"

"He changed it into understanding and gave it back to me," I answered.

"Can God really do that?" Alton asked, with just a bit of skepticism.

"Yes, God can really do that," I answered.

"Can I keep the stone, Mr. Mel?" Alton asked, holding it up in front of his face.

"Of course," I answered.

"Mr. Mel," he said, putting the stone in his pocket, "I have another problem." He hesitated for a minute or so.

211

"This is real embarrassing for me to talk about. You promise you won't get mad or laugh?"

"You can trust me, son," I said.

"Well," he said, looking away, "I'm a bed-wetter. The other kids used to laugh at me, but Mr. Pete told them that I couldn't help it. And I can't. I've tried everything. Mr. Pete even wakes me up in the middle of the night to go to the bathroom. Sometimes that helps, but most of the time it doesn't."

"Let me think on that," I said. Even though I had four children of my own, I had not been faced with this particular problem before. "Maybe once you get more control of your anger," I continued, "your problem will begin to go away. So let's work on talking to that anger. In the meantime, Mr. Pete will still wake you up every night. And before you go back to sleep, I want you to say this out loud: 'I am safe at the youth home. I am loved and cared for. No harm will come to me.' Now say it back to me."

Alton repeated the words, smiled, and ran off to join the other boys. As I watched him run up the hill, I began to understand the humility I was feeling. I truly was a part of God's plan. There was order in the universe. Purpose. Reason. God did know each of us by name. His light was bright, but not blinding. And God's light did not make shadows.

After the boys were back in their cabins, I noticed a sheet of blue paper trapped under my windshield wipers. *Not again*, I thought.

I ripped the paper from the windshield and read it: *Nigger*—

The KKK has selected you as a Point of Darkness. And you know what darkness is? Nothing.

I crumpled the paper into a ball in my hand. Then I picked up a stone and held it very, very tight. "Oh, Lord," I prayed aloud, "forgive them."

chapter twenty-three
Feeling the PRESSure

A journalist is a grumbler, a censurer, a giver of advice, a regent of sovereigns, a tutor of nations. Four hostile newspapers are more to be feared than a thousand bayonets.

Napoleon Bonaparte

C H R I S T M A S   C A M E   and went. The investigators from the state and the hostile newspaper didn't go away, though. We carried them right into the new year with us.

Sadly, despite my attempts to keep the boys in line, their attitudes were steadily declining. The boys got so out of hand that Annie was forced to suspend the writing program.

Fights broke out more often. The boys talked back to all of us without fear of retribution and often refused to cooperate, giving in only after a lengthy bargaining process.

As far as I was concerned, though, cooperation was not up for negotiation. When I was involved in the disciplinary process, cooperation was a given or the boys found themselves doing barn duty. Maybe cutting deals with children works when the children are within a normal range of behavior: children who always had love, security, and understanding, children who never went hungry. Even then, the best-behaved child, given enough rope, could easily hang himself. I always felt it was my duty as the substitute father of these boys to make sure that I didn't give them too much rope. In fact, that meant keeping most of the kids on a very short tether.

When it came to bookkeeping, I was paying for my sins, and every spare moment I had I devoted to straightening up my files. I was doing just that when Norris came pounding on the farmhouse door.

"Dad, it's me. Open up the door," he called. I could see Norris through the window. Something had upset him badly.

He walked in and threw his coat on the living-room chair. "I've had it this time! These kids just won't listen. You tell them to do something and they accuse you of humiliating them. You threaten them with some kind of punishment and they say you're abusing them. Since when did they get to vote?"

"What happened this time?" I asked.

"I told Jack to stop pushing one of the boys," muttered Norris. "And do you know what he said to me? He told me to p— off. Then that little . . . person . . . laughed. So what am I supposed to do? Report him to the social worker so she can tell the psychologist, so they can put the kid into years of therapy for his dysfunctional behavior? I'm telling you, Dad, we're not only losing the battle, we're losing the war. And another thing—I'm getting real tired of all the calls we've been getting from the Pittsburgh newspaper. I'm answering all their questions as best I can. You're gonna have to talk to them."

"You're not the only one complaining to me about Jack," I said, feeling as if I were failing the boys, "but CYS is watching me like a hawk. If I slip up, we won't get our license. I don't know what to tell you. At this point, the best you can do is note Jack's behavior in his file. Now what's this about the newspaper?"

"They're calling two and three times a week, demanding to speak with you. I keep telling them I'm able to answer any questions they have. Dad, you should hear some of the questions. It's going to take me weeks to get that information to them. Know something else? They're getting pretty nasty."

"It sounds like they're working on something big," I said. It didn't surprise me. Their reporters had been busy for months, asking questions about me. "If it's public information, get it to them as soon as you can. If it's not, don't answer them. You can handle it."

"Yeah, well, it's a pain in the butt," Norris said, grabbing his coat. "By the way, the county is lifting their 'freeze'. They'll start sending new kids next week."

"That's a bit of good news," I said. Maybe the system was beginning to trust me again.

"What's so good about it? That just means we have more kids to baby-sit." Norris walked out and slammed the door behind him.

Everyone was getting frustrated, including me, but we had to hang on and play by the rules.

I adjusted my eyeglasses and went back to my paperwork. About ten minutes after Norris left, he buzzed me on the intercom.

"Dad, the newspaper is on line one. They want to talk to you."

"Tell them I'm busy."

"I already told them that. They still want to talk to you."

"Can't you handle it?" I asked. I suppose Norris was trying to make a point.

"They don't want to talk to me."

"Norris, you handle it."

"Okay, I'll talk to them, but they'll just call back tomorrow."

And they did. As I was on my way from the barn to the farmhouse, my mind was loaded with problems. I was thinking about the newspaper and wondering what they were up to when Norris called to me from the doorway of the trailer.

"Dad!" he yelled. "Come here. I want you to take this phone call."

I walked over to the trailer and stood on the front steps.

"Well," Norris asked sarcastically, "are you coming in or should I bring the phone out to you?"

I pointed to the manure on my cowboy boots.

"Don't move," Norris ordered, signaling with his hands for me to stay put. "Carol thinks this trailer stinks enough already. I'll get the phone."

"Hold on a second," I said, scrapping some of the manure off my boots. "Who wants to talk to me?"

"The newspaper," Norris said, rolling his eyes. "They're getting pretty belligerent. Just talk to them for a couple of minutes and calm them down."

"I don't know why they need to talk to me," I said. "You've been answering their questions for the past four months. That's your job."

"And their job is to pester the Devil out of me. I swear, in their own way, this newspaper is as bad as the Klan."

"Now, Son," I murmured, "the reporters are just doing their work."

"So's the Klan," Norris grumbled. "For the last four months that paper has made over thirty calls to this place. Their list of questions keeps growing. Calling us has become part of their routine, and they've been keeping both Carol and me real busy. We can't satisfy them. Besides, I have other, more important things to do around here. They've set a deadline, and they want their questions answered by you."

"They're giving you deadlines?" I asked. I didn't like the sound of that at all.

"Yeah," Norris answered. "It's like we're on a TV quiz show. Beep! Time is up!"

"Well, I . . ."

"Dad, please," Norris interrupted. "Just talk to them. Every time they call, they ask for you. They think you're avoiding them because you have something to hide."

"Give me the phone," I said. I wasn't feeling very

generous at the moment. Reporters had been sneaking around, talking to my boys, my family, my friends, and even the guy I bought my car from. "I'll talk, but tell them I only have fifteen minutes. I've got a flight to catch."

Norris nodded, disappeared for a moment, then returned with the phone in his hands. "Hello, this is Mel Blount," I said abruptly, gripping the receiver like a weapon. "Let's not waste any time. Start asking questions."

"Hello, Mr. Blount," said a man's voice on the other end. "I'm so glad that you have decided to speak with me. We have been trying for some time to arrange an interview. You must be a very busy man, not being able to meet with us or take our calls, but, as you've probably noticed, we'll do what it takes to get our story."

"Listen, son," I said. "You're wasting time here. If you have something you want to ask me, then ask me."

"Well, Mr. Blount," he said in a soft, even tone. "We have one problem. We need far more of your time than fifteen minutes, and your son knows that. I guess he thought that if you came to the phone that would somehow appease us. But, Mr. Blount, we have some serious concerns about your management of the youth home. Since the public donates money and services to your home and trusts you with the care of their children, we believe it is in the public's best interest for you to meet with us and answer our questions.

"After all, Mr. Blount, we have been trying for a very long time to get the answers to all our questions. We can't understand why you are avoiding us or why you are making it so difficult for us to access public information. And, Mr. Blount, how you run the home and where you spend the money is public information. You are bound by law to give us the answers to our questions."

"Sir," I said, "I believe I am bound to make information 'accessible' to you. I don't believe that the information must come from me in the form of a lengthy interview.

"Carol and Norris have assured me that they're doing their best to answer your questions in what they feel is a timely manner. As you know, we've had our problems out here, what with the CYS and Legal Aid Society breathing down our backs. Your paper has done a fine job in reporting our problems, so I'm sure you're aware of the work we have ahead of us, but you may not be aware of the good that we've accomplished. Norris would be happy to show you around the home, and you can talk with the counselors and the boys, if you like."

"That won't do, Mr. Blount," he said slowly.

"Hey, if you're looking for me to admit that I've made some mistakes, I'll concede that I've made numerous mistakes, zillions of mistakes. In fact, I've already admitted that. I made mistakes in my business, my personal life, even here at the home, but that's all behind me now. God and I talked about those mistakes in great detail, and He tests me daily to see if I'll repeat those mistakes. So far, so good."

The reporter tried to interrupt me, but I had a full head of steam and wasn't about to stop. "Please . . . allow me to go on," I said. "The youth home can't afford any more problems from the press. Our last chance for a permanent license is only a couple of months away. We're working very hard here, so we comply with every regulation that the state, county, CYS, and Legal Aid Society have imposed on us. We're getting our license, too. How about we meet halfway? As soon as we get our license, we'll sit down and talk. Son, I'm just too busy now."

There was a pause. "Mr. Blount," the man said. "That was a good speech. I see that you've inherited your father's persuasive powers and your grandfather's shrewdness. But we still need for you to answer our questions. If you refuse to cooperate, we are going to have to make other, less amiable arrangements."

"What's this about my dad and grandpa?" I was so flustered I almost dropped the phone onto the ground. "I beg your pardon? Persuasive? Shrewd? How would you know what my dad and grandpa were like? You never knew them."

"I may have never met them, but I know them," he said smugly. "And I know you, too."

I wasn't about to discuss my family with this man. From his words and manner, I was learning more about him than I cared to know. "If I'm hearing you correctly," I said, staring down at my dirty boots, "I'd say that as far as your newspaper is concerned, I'm standing knee-deep in a pile of horse manure."

"Look at it any way you like, Mr. Blount," he said, chuckling slightly. "But I do like your description of the situation. Sort of fits you."

We said our courtesy good-byes and I hung up the phone. I tapped on the window and called to Norris.

"Well?" he asked, taking the phone from my hand. "How did it go?"

"I wish I could wash away the newspaper as easily as I can wash the manure from my boots."

Norris laughed. "You're going to need a mighty big hose. And even if you managed to rinse away the dirt, the newspaper would still stink to high heaven."

Of that I had no doubt.

• • •

I arrived back home after spending a few days on the road with the NFL. As I was pulling my bags from the trunk of my car, Carol shouted from the window of the trailer. "We've been recommended for our permanent license."

I raised my arms above my head in victory. That was great news. Even though I didn't find working with the system pleasurable, we had scored a touchdown, and now we were in the lead again.

I walked down to the trailer to congratulate Carol, but when I opened the door and saw Jack Langley, one of our board members, sitting at the kitchen table, the thrill of victory fizzled out of me.

"Carol said it would be okay if I waited here for you," Jack said, fingering the salt shaker.

"Have you been waiting long?" I asked, setting my bags down.

"An hour or so," Carol answered for him.

"Well, you must have something real important you want to talk about. Let's go back to my office."

"No, Mel, this will only take a minute. The Pittsburgh newspaper wants you to meet with them," Jack began, "and I'm here to ask you to do it."

"That's what's so important?" I asked. "You know, I already agreed to meet with them in June."

"Mel, that's two months away. They won't wait that long."

"What's so important about meeting earlier?" I asked. "I respect the newspaper's right to do a story, but I've been busy. We've just been recommended for our permanent license, and I have to get ready for the inspection committee."

"Mel, if you don't agree to meet with them now, they are going to start doing articles on the board members. All of them. One by one. And guess who they're going to start with? Me."

"Who told you that?" I asked, making sure that I was getting a clear picture of what was going on.

"The paper," he answered. "When a newspaper warns you that they are going to do an article about you, I think you can safely assume that it isn't going to be complimentary. I believe I have been warned."

"What can they possibly say bad about you?" I asked. "What are you, twenty-eight, twenty-nine years old?"

"Thirty."

"Okay, thirty. What evil thing did you ever do? Cheat on a test once?" This was getting crazy.

"Their intention isn't to drag out whatever skeletons are hanging in my closet. They're going to blame all of us for the problems at the home. 'You are the board, so you are ultimately responsible;' that's what they're going to say. My law partners are very upset, and I can't blame them. We're a new firm. We can't risk any bad publicity, and neither can any of the board members."

"I am responsible for everything around here," I assured him. "If a counselor hits a kid, I'm the one accused of wrongdoing. If the bills don't get paid, it's me they'll come after. I'll take responsibility."

"Well, to do that, you're going to have to meet with the newspaper." He picked up a paper napkin and tore it into strips. "Throw yourself at their mercy. Plead to their better half. Do cartwheels if they ask you to. Why do you think they're called the press? They carry enough weight to flatten an elephant. Talk to them before they really start to hurt you."

"I'll meet with them. I don't like being pressured, but I'll meet with them."

"Thanks, Mel." I could see the relief on his face. "I'm certain you'll be able straighten things out with the newspaper. Maybe they'll even start liking you again."

"You really believe that?" I asked.

"No, I don't" he answered flatly. "I think you're in deep and serious trouble with them.

"So do I," I agreed, "but I might as well start walking through the fire. Last time I checked, that was the only way to get through to the other side."

chapter twenty-four
DePRESS

The tongue of the slanderer is brother to the dagger of the assassin.
Tryon Edwards

T H E N E W S P A P E R ' S tactics verged on harassment. At least, that's what my attorney said. I had to admit, I was feeling harassed, but I had been under a great deal of pressure. I kept reminding myself that *coal under pressure becomes a diamond.*

If the newspaper's attitude was the only problem I had to take care of, I probably wouldn't have felt so stressed. But I was still getting plenty of threats from the KKK, and contributions continued to drop. Every time I thought I was finally going to crack into little pieces, the Lord gave me more strength.

We notified the newspaper that I had agreed to meet with them, but I had some conditions. I didn't want any tape recorders or cameras. There were to ask no personal questions, and I didn't want to be interviewed by the reporter who had been interviewing the boys, my family, and friends. I told the newspaper that that guy was incapable of any fair and balanced reporting where I was concerned. I wanted to meet with the top editors. I figured they were the ones responsible for the stories on me, so they should meet face-to-face with the man they were bent on destroying. And I wanted a written list of questions they were going to ask so I could prepare answers for them. I didn't want to spend more than an hour on questions from the newspaper. As far as I was concerned, I had already spent too much time on them.

It was a warm spring day, and I was in the mood to visit my mountaintop. I didn't have anything I wanted to complain about or ask for. I just wanted to check in with the Lord.

I was just about to slip the bridle over Wind's head when Norris found me. "The newspaper called. They aren't very happy. The editor and managing editor have refused to meet with you, and they won't give you a written list of questions because they're afraid their story will fall prey to their competition."

"What does that mean?" I asked.

"I don't know. Maybe they think we'll give the list to another newspaper or something."

"Maybe they're afraid that list will be used as evidence against them."

"Who knows?" Norris said, patting Wind's neck. "Anyway, they're really upset that you've only given them an hour and no tape recorders. They said that was too restrictive. I guess now they'll have to write out your answers. And the reporter you don't want? Well, they want to use him. They say he's been working on the story for months."

"If they send him, I'll tell my attorney not to let him in the room. I'm serious. I don't want to see that guy."

"Okay, Dad. I'm setting it up for tomorrow afternoon."

"That's fine with me."

Norris started to walk away, then stopped and turned around. "By the way, the City of Pittsburgh has named March third 'Mel Blount Day.' Seems like someone down there likes you."

"That's real nice of them." That was the Pittsburgh I knew.

• • •

I met with the newspaper, but nothing much came out of the meeting, so I arranged to give them another interview the following week. But I insisted on that list. They were reluctant but promised to send it to us. That's when Norris hit the roof.

I was about to get into the youth-home van when Norris tracked me down. "We've got to talk."

"Can it wait until I get back?" I asked. "I have to get to town before the bank closes."

"I'll go with you," Norris said, opening the passenger door and climbing in beside me. This had to be serious, I thought. Norris hates my driving.

"I got the newspaper's questions today," Norris said, holding them up for me to see. "The board members got a copy of the list, too. If we don't answer these, the board members will have to."

"So let's get them answered," I said, stopping at an intersection.

"Dad, you know that nothing having to do with the youth home is that easy. Some of these questions date back to . . . I don't even know when. There's one here about the youth home in Georgia. How can we find out exactly what happened down there in 1988 on such short notice? Some of these questions are based on interviews you gave to the press two and three years ago."

"Can we get the answers?"

"I guess so," Norris answered, "but it's going to take more than a week to find them. Question number sixty-three is especially nasty. They're asking about the terms of your divorce and implying you started the youth home to hide some assets."

"Good Lord Almighty! Merciful Father in heaven!" I clenched my fingers so tightly around the steering wheel that my knuckles grew pale.

"And you know what really has me upset, Dad? They're accusing me of paddling the boys. Next thing I know, they'll probably be hauling me to court on child-abuse charges." Norris was not only upset, he was scared. If I were his age and I had my whole life ahead of me, I would have been reacting the same way. Norris, of all people, had a gentle heart. He'd never lift a hand against a child. This accusation was crushing him.

"They're using you to get to me," I said, reaching over and touching him on the arm, "but don't worry. I won't let them do that."

"I won't let them either, Dad, because I want to resign."

We drove on in silence for a little while. "I have to protect my family," Norris said, tapping on the window with his finger. "They come first. If the newspaper starts after me, then what? I'm not going to put Denitia and the girls through this."

"You have to do what you think is right," I said, pulling off to the side of the road. I looked him in the eye. "Get all your ducks in a row first. Talk to Denitia, find another job, take it one step at a time."

"Well, that makes sense. The only thing is, I hate having to leave you just now when you need so much help."

"I do need you, Norris, but I won't try to keep you here," I said. I would have liked to, but I knew it would be wrong even to try.

We reached the bank, and after I finished my business there, Norris and I stopped for pie at a local diner. As I sat watching him eat his second piece of apple pie, I knew that I would fight to the death for him. The newspaper could shoot all the bullets they wanted at me, but they'd best be leaving my boy alone.

I also knew that, no matter whether I answered all the questions or none at all, the article about me was already written.

When we got back to the youth home, I made a few calls, explaining to some friends, my attorney, and a couple of local councilmen what I thought was happening. I read some of the questions and told them how long the newspaper's investigation had been going on. Their response was always the same. "Sue 'em."

Somehow that just didn't seem right, but I promised to keep it under consideration. They all agreed to meet with me at my attorney's office the following afternoon to help me decide how I should deal with the newspaper.

Throughout the evening, all I kept hearing from everyone was "sue 'em." By the time I went to bed, I was convinced that it was the only thing I could do.

chapter twenty-five
Embracing the Enemy

God hears no more than the heart speaks; and if the heart be dumb,
God will certainly be deaf.

Thomas Brooks

I S T O O D A L O N E in the boardroom, staring out
the window to the rivers below. The bridges were filled with
traffic as people made their way to and from the city. I
remembered the day I arrived in Pittsburgh, nearly twenty
years ago. A lot sure had changed, for both the city and me.
The smokestacks that puffed black soot into the air were
gone, and Pittsburgh was no longer the city of steel.

Well, I thought, *I had really become a Pittsburgher.* I
complained about the back-up of traffic at the Squirrel Hill
Tunnels, spoke Pittsburghese—with a Georgia accent—and
I knew what an Iron City Light was. I was even beginning to
like Pittsburgh winters.

I smiled as I remembered the first time I asked a native
for directions to an office building downtown, which I was
having trouble finding. He looked at me for a moment,
started to explain, then decided it was easier and a sight
more neighborly to take me there himself.

I belonged here. I was no longer a stranger. Pittsburgh
knew me, and I knew Pittsburgh. The people here are not

my enemies. They're good people. I knew what it was like to have them cheer me on, and I've felt the sting of their disappointment. I've given them my best, and they've rewarded me very well.

I was proud of Pittsburgh. Its spirit was as hard as steel. When the mills closed, the city adapted to the changes. It moved on, even though the adaptation was painful and full of hardships. And that's what I needed to do—move on.

As I was wondering exactly what that would mean for me, I felt the hand of God move me and I knew what I must do. A feeling of peace, gentle and comforting, opened my eyes to the answer that had been in front of me the whole time. I put my hand to the window and touched the city.

"Mel," I heard a voice behind me. "You're not thinking of jumping, are you?"

"Annie," I said, turning around. "Glad you could make it."

"I wouldn't miss this 'meeting of the minds' for anything. Let's see . . . you have a public relations expert, two very good lawyers, some board members, a council-man, and a partridge in a pear tree," she said pointing to herself, "and all of us are going to help you make a decision. Dollars to doughnuts, you already know what you're going to do. And I'll just bet you that no one in this room will agree with you. Including me."

I didn't get a chance to comment because the partici-pants in the meeting began filing into the room. After a brief exchange of pleasantries, we sat down to business.

I listened to everyone. The lawyers wanted me to sue the newspaper. The public relations man wanted me to start a "positive campaign" to counteract the negative publicity. The board members wanted me to do both. And the councilman advised me to "make a deal."

The talking went back and forth for almost two hours, and I listened patiently while they were deciding my fate. I couldn't remember a time when I stayed quiet for so long, especially when I was the topic of discussion. Finally, everyone agreed on one thing: It was time for me to make a decision.

I stood up and cleared my throat. "You're all very kind for meeting with me today. That list of questions you have before you has many shades of gray that are missing from it. I've admitted over and over that I've made some mistakes, but you all know me and the work I'm doing. More important, *I* know me and the work I'm doing."

I paused for a few minutes and cleared my throat again. I knew that what I had to say next would not be very popular. "This is the Lord's youth home, not mine. Since that's the fact of the matter, I had to ask myself, 'What would the Lord want me to do?' Actually, until a little while ago, I didn't know for sure what was right, but I know now. It's simply this—I'm giving up the fight. I'm not going to do battle with the newspaper.

"My job is to build a solid foundation for the youth home. The newspaper's job is to print articles. My youth home can't stop their presses any more than their presses can stop my youth home, at least not without the consent of a power much greater than mine or that of the editors. I have a feeling, though, that the loaded cannon they think they're aiming at me is really aimed at themselves. I'd say people are getting pretty tired of reading about me, and what we all think is negative press really isn't.

"Anyway, regardless of what happens, I can't let myself get sidetracked from what I set out to do. When I played football, I played the position of cornerback. I didn't try to play quarterback, I didn't try to coach, I didn't try selling peanuts to the fans. I did my job, and that's what I'm going to get back to doing. The time I threatened to sue the Steelers was an awful angry and painful time for me. I don't want to go through that again. I just wanted to play football then. I just want to run the youth home now.

"I once asked the Lord to make me a great football player. You have no idea what the Lord put me through, because becoming the best isn't easy. The first challenge the

Lord sent me was Cliff Branch, but I won't get into that story here.

"I asked the Lord for greatness for the youth home. I wanted a program that really worked, and I wanted the children to come first. From what I've seen of child care within the system, the children usually come last, so I knew I had to step out of the system to reach my goal. My struggle isn't with the newspaper—it's with the system. That's clear to me now.

"Because I had to prove that what I'm doing at the home is worthy and can stand up to the test, the Lord sent me challenges: the CYS, the Department of Public Welfare, the Legal Aid Society, the Klan, the newspaper, the Concerned Citizens, and many others. I believe that I will find little rest if I intend to keep doing the Lord's work.

"I didn't know at first why I was being sent so many obstacles, but those people helped define me and the home. Those people really did me a favor, just like Cliff Branch, because they helped me to focus on my game.

"A pastor once told me, 'You'd better really want what you ask the Lord to give you.' All I can say is, he sure knew what he was talking about. And if that wise pastor were here today, I'm pretty sure he would tell me to 'embrace my enemies.' So I'm going to embrace my enemy."

"What do you mean by that, Mel?" Annie asked.

"I'm going to call the paper and offer to meet with them, just to talk. Then I'll tell them to do what they feel they have to do."

"They're not going to meet with you," my lawyer said, shaking his head.

"So be it."

I dialed the newspaper's number. After some hemming and hawing and buck-passing, I got my answer plain and simple: They refused to meet with me.

My advisors made a few comments. It was clear to see that most of them were very disappointed and had little faith in my decision.

Everyone left the room as downcast as a team that has

lost the big game. Only Annie lingered behind. "Tell me, who do you think you are, Gandhi?"

I laughed. "I did the right thing, you know," I said, satisfied that I was finished waging a war. I had never wanted to fight.

"I know you did."

Annie left the room, and once again I was alone.

• • •

As fate would have it, the newspaper finally did agree to meet with me. We talked about many things, although I'm sure whatever I had to say for myself had little impact on what they eventually printed. They ran articles in Monday's and Tuesday's paper, a two-part series, about six pages, complete with photographs. Three reporters wrote it. As we had expected, our phones began to ring.

But what no one expected, including me, was the show of support for me and the youth home. The reaction from the local townsfolk and the public in general was almost the same as it had been after the Klan's cross-burning. "Why don't they just leave you alone and get on to something else?" a caller said. "This picking on you is beginning to get on my nerves. How do you people at the home put up with this stuff and still manage to get up and go to work?"

Contributions increased, morale picked up, supporters rallied. The articles had backfired. But the newspaper wasn't done firing at me.

"Mel," Annie said over the phone, "did you read tonight's editorial?"

"Nope," I answered, "I haven't been reading the paper much lately."

"Well, listen to this." I could hear the glee in Annie's voice. "A desirable characteristic in a chief executive officer is the ability to see the big picture and to act on that vision, while delegating to others the necessary detail work. Less desirable is the person whose pursuit of the dream is so consuming that details, no matter how necessary, are brushed aside.

" 'To our dismay, we have found that Mel Blount, football hero and founder of a Washington County home for boys, may be assigned to the latter category.

" 'The discovery was anything but sudden. It was the result of months of digging by a team of reporters who looked—as far as they could—into the workings of the Mel Blount Youth Home. . . .' "

"It goes on to say that your football days are but a memory and the youth home is now your identity, then recounts the problems you've had. The facility is 'superb' and expensive. They've agreed for the most part that you've made honest mistakes, but say you are far too cavalier in your care of the children and that you've initiated change only because of the pressure of the government and because of the public questions you've had to answer. Of course, you and I both know who took it upon themselves to ask those 'public questions.' "

"Well," I said, "little do they know we've been changing and adjusting since day one and will continue to do that every day that these doors stay open."

"If you're lucky, they'll stay open for a long time," Annie replied, "because, according to the paper, you've only gotten this far because you're a very, very lucky man." She knew that would get to me.

"I don't believe in luck," I said, "as you well know. I believe in hard work. Doing a job. Luck! You know, that really makes me mad. I don't ever want to send a message to our kids that success is a result of luck. No one, I don't care how many newspapers they own, should even imply that luck has anything to do with success."

"You know something? I think the paper got a lot of flack about those articles on you," Annie said knowingly.

"Why's that?"

"Because they felt they had to try to justify the articles by publishing an editorial two weeks later."

"Thanks for telling me about it, Annie," I said, "but you know, I'm not even going to read it. The battle's over and I don't want to look at the pictures of the dead." *Maybe*, I thought, *that cannon really is pointed at the newspaper now.*

chapter twenty-six
Jack Throws Stones

Anger is as a stone cast into a wasp's nest.

Malabar Proverb

I THOUGHT I deserved a day to myself, so I decided
to play hookey from my work at the home. The Department
of Public Welfare found the Legal Aid Society's accusations
to be unfounded; the newspaper article was printed and
discarded with the trash; and we had received our permanent license. We had done good.

I saddled Tomahawk and we headed for the back
acreage. The air smelled sweet with the aroma that shouted,
"planting season." To a farmer, there was only one smell
that was better: the rich scent of the harvest.

I stopped long enough to check out the freshly plowed
fields and was satisfied that we would have a good growing
season, provided the weather cooperated. It wasn't often in
this part of the country that our crops were burned out. One
thing I really like about Pennsylvania is its soil; it sure is
black and rich. Of course, it couldn't grow onions like the
onions in Vidalia, Georgia, but, to a farmer—and I still had
a farmer's blood pumping through my veins—what mattered was that I was planting something.

As I rode, I had time to reflect on the fact that Norris

234

had left the home earlier that week. Although by now the home had its share of comings and goings, this going was the hardest for me. My own son, was out on his own, facing the world with a wife, two children, and a new job in a different state. It was a gentle good-bye. No tears. No regrets. We shook hands the stiff, formal way that men do, and we wished each other a good life. I missed him.

I saw my neighbor in the field, waved to him, and called hello. He ignored me. One of us, I was sure, would eventually have to give in and move, and I knew it wouldn't be me.

I rode the length of the fence, inspecting it for broken or loose rails. One section of the fence was down; my guess was that it had been deliberately damaged. We had a slight problem with people on trail bikes removing sections of the fence. For the most part, though, the fence looked ship-shape.

It had been months since I felt so relaxed. At one point, I got off my horse and lay down in the grass, staring at the sky. The ground still had some warming up to do, but its coolness felt good to me. I put a blade of grass in my mouth and chewed on it. For the first time in a long while, my mind was clear of trouble and conflict. New ideas began flooding my head. I knew that I needed more time like this.

When the sun began getting low in the sky, I decided to head back to the farm and check in with Carol before she left for the day. I knew she would greet me with a list of phone calls to be returned and a stack of mail for me to read.

"I hope you're well-rested," she said, walking in from the kitchen as I entered the trailer. "The counselors are really having a problem with Jack. Mel, the kid is totally out of control. Just the other day he swore at me. That child has the mouth of a sailor, and he doesn't have the slightest bit of respect for anything or anyone."

This was nothing new. There were so many complaints about Jack's behavior that I felt certain we were going to lose him. Either he would have to straighten out or leave the program. Keeping peace and order was hard enough with all the restrictions that had been placed upon us. We just didn't have room for boys who failed to improve.

It was obvious to me that the system's way of dealing with Jack's problem—that is, ignoring it—was not going to work. So, I had a choice: talk with him myself or request that he be removed. I felt I only had one option, to take matters into my own hands. I now knew what I would do when the rules got in the way of helping a child.

"Carol," I said, gulping down a glass of water. "I'm going to have a talk with that boy."

"I don't think that's a good idea," Carol warned.

"What do you suggest?"

"Maybe some other facility would be better for him," Carol offered.

"And where would that facility be?" I asked. "Grandville?"

"At least have a counselor present when you talk to him," she answered, "so there's no misunderstandings on anyone's part."

I didn't bother changing my riding clothes. I headed straight to Cabin One to meet with Jack. He was sitting in the living room, reading a comic book.

"Get over here, boy," I said, not noticing if a counselor was present or not. "And move quick 'cause I'm feeling none too patient right now." I knew that I might be subjecting myself to more condemnation from the system, but at that moment I didn't care. Only Jack's welfare mattered to me.

Jack slowly walked toward me, staring at me with a look of defiance that grew bolder with every step.

"What do you want?" he demanded.

"I hear from the counselors that you're causing all kinds of trouble here, and I want you to explain yourself to me." I looked down at him. The boy wasn't any taller than my chest. "And," I warned, rather strongly, "your explanation better be good, 'cause son, I'm tired of hearing about you all the time."

"I don't have to explain myself to you or anybody else," he said with a snicker, turning away from me. I knew linebackers that stood six-foot-five, weighing over two hundred pounds, in top physical condition, who would not have dared to stand in front of me with the disrespect this child was showing me.

"Listen, boy, I'm not gonna take that lip from you. I'm not asking you to explain yourself. I'm *telling* you." I took his arm and turned him around.

"You got no business telling me anything," he said, raising his fist to me. "So get out of my face, you stupid nigger."

"You just crossed over the line, son," I growled, pointing my finger in his face. I walked toward him, and he backed away from me until he bumped up against the wall. "What did you say? I don't think I heard you right the first time."

"Nigger!" he shouted, pushing my hand away and slipping by me. "You're in big trouble now," he screamed, as he ran back toward his room.

I stood stock-still in disbelief. All I could think of was my own dad. Had I done something like this, I wouldn't be able to sit for a week, and deservedly so. But, according to CYS, I had to allow Jack to get away with this display of contempt in the name of rehabilitation. I wasn't blaming the child. He was angry. That was a normal response for a child who had been abandoned. He had never known anyone he could rely on. He made it this far on his own, and the only person he trusted was himself. He was so angry and out of control that I couldn't even get his attention long enough to tell him my stone story.

Jack wasn't that much different from most of the boys who came to the home. It used to be that, until I got their trust, the boys feared me enough to listen. Once I got their attention, the fear disappeared and I earned their love and respect. They came to understand why I held them account-able for their actions. It would have been far easier, of course, to allow the kids to do whatever they wanted, then just close my eyes and walk away. But then I would have had to live with the fact that I'd allowed a child to drown in a sea of apathy, and I couldn't do that.

No sooner did that incident with Jack happen than I was once again suspected of child abuse. The media reported that "Mel Blount is back in the news again as more accusations of mistreating the boys are made."

Jack had told his social worker that I had thrown him against the wall and threatened his life. I had violated the orders that forbade me to discipline the boys, and I knew it. Once again, by my own choice, I had broken the rules, not because I like breaking rules, but because they simply were not working. I had no idea what my punishment would be, but I knew I would be punished.

I knew that the system would hold me accountable. But who the devil holds the system accountable?

The system should be like a farmer taking care of his wheat, namely, the children. That farmer should be watering his wheat and helping it grow, and if he lets that wheat field go to weed, then he should be held responsible. Instead, the public goes right on pretending that weeds are wheat and paying wheat prices for weed quality. My dad would never tolerate that kind of farming . . . and I won't tolerate that kind of child care. It isn't right, it isn't just, and it's destroying our children, the precious seeds of our future.

There are all sorts of examples of the system's failure to be a good farmer. Annie told me about one foster family down in Texas who tried to adopt a little girl, but the system returned the poor child to her abusive mother instead. The youngster nearly died, and would have, if her foster parents hadn't fought for her custody. And right here in Pittsburgh, a little boy was killed by his foster father because the system refused to remove the child, even though there was plenty of evidence that his life was in danger.

Who holds the system accountable for all these disasters and near-disasters? Well, I do, for one. Just because the system is a bad farmer, doesn't mean I have to be. And where Jack was concerned, I only wished to harvest wheat, not weeds.

chapter twenty-seven
Three Strikes, You're Out

I want to thank every one who made this day necessary.

Yogi Berra

Pro football is like nuclear warfare. There are no winners, only survivors.

Frank Gifford

W H E N   T H E   N E W S   of my continuing struggles was broadcast, the local talk shows began calling to invite me to appear on their programs. I turned down the "opportunity" to tell my side of the story. I almost found it laughable that one program, involving the editors of the newspaper, would have pitted me against Ms. Forte, the attorney of the Legal Aid Society. I suppose they thought it would be amusing to watch a lawyer and me involved in a legal dispute on the air. Whether it was for entertainment or to truly inform the public, I simply was not going to allow myself to fall prey to any situation that could have harmed the home. In fact, I didn't think that anyone in his right mind would talk with the opposition, especially a lawyer.

The editors were very upset that I had declined to do the show. They simply couldn't understand why I didn't want to meet with Ms. Forte. If they had only known about the battles we had waged during the past year, the editors would not have even bothered wondering why. Ms. Forte was only doing her job. I understood that. I was to the point, though, that I didn't care too much for her attitude toward me or the boys, who were, after all, her clients.

Once again, Ann Devlin came to my aid. She asked me to appear on her show and respond to the media's attacks on the home. One of her staff members assured me that they were on my side and couldn't understand why I wasn't allowed to do my job in peace. I declined as graciously as I could.

I was content to have the Department of Public Welfare do their investigation because I knew that, in the end, they would call my treatment of Jack corporal punishment, not abuse. I wasn't sure what the consequences would be, but I was willing to take whatever they dished out.

I had suspected, though, after a talk with the director of the home, that I had played into their hands and was headed for some serious trouble. The conversation between us was brief and to the point. Basically, he implied that I should have minded my own business—which I thought I was doing—and allowed the counselors to handle Jack.

"Mel, the Department of Public Welfare told me that if it weren't for me, there would be no program here," the director said, without any hesitation at all. I had chosen this man as director of my youth home at the strong recommendation of the Department of Public Welfare because of his experience with the ins and outs of the system. That was good, I believed. We needed someone who knew how to tactfully handle the bureaucracy. But that wasn't the case. He was pushing me out.

Now I understood. They believed that I was expendable, extra weight that was bogging down the system. They were trying to rid themselves of me. The director gave no consideration to the fact that I had started this place, that I was the one who held a mortgage for 1.5 million dollars and was the one on the firing line day after day. My life had been threatened, the newspaper had tried to publicly humiliate me, and I was constantly battling to raise enough money to keep this place going. Just a few hours prior to that conversation with the director, I practically had to beg a businesswoman for a donation so that I could meet the mortgage on the farm, while the director sat in his office, reading charts. His arrogance made me mad, but I didn't show it. I just smiled and walked out the door. I wasn't going to react to this. I was going to *act*.

I took a short walk around the farm. After stopping in at the cabins and saying hello to the boys, I went to the farmhouse to have dinner.

Between her work and mine, TiAnda and I didn't have much time together, so I decided not to burden her with my new set of problems. I just wanted us to enjoy a nice, quiet dinner together, free from interruption. The phone rang as we were sitting down to eat.

"Mel," Annie said, "turn on your TV. You're being discussed on a local talk show." She quickly gave me the channel number and hung up the phone.

Did I really want to turn the television on? I asked myself. I knew that if I did, it would be the end of the evening I had planned to spend with my wife. My peace and quiet would be interrupted, and I didn't know when I would find it again.

I turned on the television.

Across the bottom of the screen I read: "Mel Blount on Defense." I hoped that this was going to be a review of some old game films, but I knew better than that. The host began by having a staff reporter from the newspaper speak. He said that I was, for the second time, being accused of abusing the boys. When it came time for her to speak, the attorney from the Legal Aid Society quickly corrected the reporter, explaining that what I had done was considered corporal punishment and that my actions did not meet the state guidelines for abuse. *Great*, I thought, *anyone who had tuned out before hearing that correction will think I have abused my boys.*

"Basically," said the lawyer, "the only time a counselor

may touch a child is when there is a need for passive restraint. What Mr. Blount did goes beyond that definition."

"Some of our own staff have asked why you are picking on Mel Blount," said the staff reporter. "They say these kids are no good. Spare the rod, spoil the child, so to speak."

"That's a misconception about the boys," the attorney argued. "These are not delinquent children, they are dependent children who have been removed from their parents' care and control. They were abused in their homes—some sexually, others physically. The last thing they need is to suffer any more emotional trauma."

I started talking to the television screen. "I can't believe what you're saying about me!" On second thought, I should have expected it.

"Is the home successful?" the host of the program asked.

"There's no way we can measure that. Some kids succeed, some don't. The Mel Blount Youth Home is only two years old. The success of that program can't be measured. We don't know the long-term effects."

"How does the state decide if the facility or program is good for the child?" the host inquired.

"Licensing standards are governed through strict regulations," said the lawyer. "That's why the state sends monitors to ensure that the home is being run according to those guidelines. There's a whole array of programs available, and no particular program works one-hundred percent of the time."

"So tell them how hard we worked to get our license. Tell them we're state approved," I said, throwing my hands in the air.

"Is there a difference between boys' and girls' programs?" the host probed.

"A big difference," the attorney answered. "With girls, the emphasis is on self-image. With boys, it's on behavioral modifications—how to not be so aggressive and to express their anger in a more acceptable way."

"That's what I was doing," I said in my defense. "That's why they exercise and clean out stalls."

"How many times are you willing to give Mr. Blount a consent order?" the staff reporter asked.

"Well, let's put it this way—three strikes, you're out. Mr. Blount already has two."

What does that mean? I asked myself. *Are they going to make me leave the home? And what's this "three strikes, you're out" stuff? Get with the game.*

● ● ●

TiAnda and I were on our way to the car for a rare trip to the movies when one of the counselors came running over to me.

"Mel," he said, a little out of breath, "Jack has been out of control all day. He's been threatening to commit suicide. I know you're on your way out, but I just thought you would like to know about this."

"Have him put under twenty-four-hour watch and make sure that he's not left alone for even one second," I ordered. "How bad off do you really think he is?"

"With that kid, it's hard to say for sure," the counselor answered, taking a deep breath. "This whole situation has been difficult for all the kids. I think Jack is going through a tough period of adjustment, just like some of the other boys went through. Too bad we can't have him doing something to wear off all that aggression. But, Mel, I could be wrong. I don't have to tell you how crazy things have been around this place since this investigation crap started. Sometimes I just don't know who's in charge."

"Do the best you can," I said, getting into the car. "I'll check in with you as soon as I get back. Don't let anything happen to that kid. Remember, don't leave him unsupervised for any reason, not even for an instant."

"Don't worry," the counselor promised, "we won't."

As I drove off, I got to thinking. Although I didn't believe that Jack was any worse off than the rest of the kids

243

and I was pretty sure we could handle his threat, I simply couldn't take the risk of keeping him at the home any longer. We found that most of the boys usually threaten to kill themselves or one of us at one point or another, often when they're in a fit of anger or because they were told to do something that they didn't want to do. We make it through the night, keep a close eye on them for a few days, and usually the boy settles down.

But what if Jack were serious? What if he did commit suicide? I didn't think it would happen, and neither did the counselors, but what if we were wrong? It was a risk that I was unwilling to take.

"What's on your mind?" TiAnda asked. "You've been too quiet."

"I was just thinking about Jack." I answered, turning the wipers on as a few drops of rain struck the windshield. A few moments later, we were driving through a rainstorm. "I'm going to have him removed from the home and taken to a hospital."

"Why? We've been through this before with the other boys," TiAnda said, surprised at my decision. "It's not like you to give up so easily."

"I haven't been allowed to get to know Jack like I have the other boys." The roads were getting slippery, and I slowed down to negotiate a curve. "I don't think I have a choice. I can't make guesses about this child's intentions. What if he stays here and we're wrong? What if he does kill himself? No one wants to see something like that happen. I'd never be able to forgive myself, and that would be the end of the program. The home would be suspect. I don't even want to think about the accusations that would be made against me. I'm making the right decision, TiAnda. At least, under these circumstances. The boy is going to be checked into the psychiatric ward."

Within a week, Jack was taken from the home and placed in a mental hospital. I wasn't sure when or even if he would be allowed to return to us. He was an angry young man, too angry to change his attitude. I never had a chance to use my type of therapy on Jack: the trail-blazing, the horseback rides, the prayer meetings, the tiny bits of my sometimes awkward philosophies. All I could do was hope that he would find, within the white walls of the hospital, the grace of God and the blessing of inner peace.

chapter twenty-eight
The Vision Realized

Christianity does not remove you from the world and its problems; it makes you fit to live in it, triumphantly and usefully.

Charles Templeton

M O M M A   W A S   coming to visit. I had been doing some work at the Georgia youth home when I decided to ask her to make the drive back north with me. She had declined every other offer I'd ever made to have her visit the Taylorstown home, and I was beginning to think that she didn't want anything to do with a Yankee state.

"Momma," I said, "your foot is nearly all better. There's nothing keeping you here. Why not drive back to Pittsburgh with me? I want to share with you all the things I've been doing up there." I half expected her to make up some excuse not to come, but she surprised me.

"Certainly, child," she said. "I would like that."

"That's great!" I couldn't believe that Momma was actually agreeing to make the trip, but soon I was helping her pack her suitcase, and the next thing I knew we were on the road together, heading north.

I was used to the long trip and usually stopped only when I absolutely had to, but with Momma in the car, I was in no hurry. I didn't want the circulation in her foot to go bad again, so I stopped nearly every chance I got.

As we drove, I'd occasionally glance over at her. No matter how old I was, I was still my momma's child. She was security, goodness, love, ideal Christianity—everything that was positive in my life. I hoped she would approve of what her son had done at the youth home in Taylorstown, although I knew it wasn't easy to impress my momma.

It was dark when we arrived. TiAnda had Momma's room ready, and after a light supper, she went to bed. But bright and early the next morning I heard Momma down in the kitchen, getting breakfast started.

"Good morning, Son," she said to me as I entered the kitchen. "I was thinking. After we finish up our meal, I would like to have a personal tour around this place. I want to meet some of the boys and see those horses I hear so much about."

How long I had waited to show her my vision that had finally been realized! And here she was, asking to see it!

Slowly, we walked around the grounds. Momma stopped and talked to everyone that passed by. She walked into the barn ahead of me with a couple of the boys who were proudly showing her around. As I was about to join them, I saw Annie's car winding its way up the youth-home drive. She beeped the horn, waved, then pulled up alongside of me. "I heard your mother's visiting," she said, rolling down her window. "I had to come and meet the woman responsible for making you." That's when I noticed the small, gold cross she was wearing around her neck. Her eyes followed my gaze.

"Oh, this," she said, touching the cross with her fingers. "I used to wear it when I was a kid."

"And?" I questioned.

"And," Annie said, smiling, "after the prayer meeting, I did some praying on my own, and suddenly I thought I heard Jesus asking me to trust Him. I realized I was being guided by a force greater than myself, and the moment that happened, I felt I had come home again."

"Welcome home." I leaned over and gave her a kiss on the forehead.

"I'd like to talk with you more about this," said Annie, "but for now, I'd love to meet your mother."

The Lord sure is filled with wonders. I was now certain that He never forgot one single star's name. I rejoiced that Annie was once again a part of the Lord's family.

I pointed to the barn. Annie's visit was short—not too much more than a quick hello. "I don't want to take any time away from you two," she said, waving good-bye.

The sun was bright and warm as we continued our tour. I helped Momma into the youth-home van and headed up the hillside. "I've got something I want to show you," I told her.

I stopped at the top of the hill. "Look," I said, pointing to the cabins below. "A couple of years ago, I saw those cabins just as they are now. Of course, they were all in my mind back then, but I did see them, and I made them real. And look over there. The building that's under construction is the administration building. The person standing there looking at it is Carol, the lady I keep telling you about. In a way, it's her building. She must check on those poor workers ten times a day."

Momma didn't say anything, but I didn't expect her to.

"On the ground where we're standing now, I'm going to build a compound big enough for a real dining hall for the boys, a meeting hall, and a library."

Momma listened silently.

"There's one more place I want you to see," I said, starting up the van. It was a bumpy ride, and Momma held tight onto the sides of the seat. After a few minutes, we arrived at my mountaintop.

"This is where I come to pray," I explained, helping her out of the van. We stood together in silence as we looked at Taylorstown.

"What a nice-looking little town," Momma said, inhaling the sweet summer air. "I should think that the people there are proud to have you be a part of it."

"I hope so," I answered. I felt that I was finally beginning to be accepted by those nice folks.

"I'm not used to all these mountains," Momma said, looking out over the valley. "They must have to work real hard plowing these fields. But I like it here. The air smells good, the earth looks downright fertile, and the trees are old and wise. I'd say the Lord has led you to a little piece of heaven."

"It sure looks that way," I agreed. Momma didn't know all of the struggles that had gone into making this place a 'little piece of heaven.'

"Child, come here. Stand close by me." She took my hand and held it tightly in hers. "Now tell me, Son, where was that cross-burning held?"

I pointed to the hillside across the valley. She raised her arms out to her sides and prayed. "Dear Mighty Father in Heaven, you set your own Son upon a cross that burns with goodness and light. It sheds understanding and love upon your children, but some of your children have turned away from you and have used that cross to spread fear and hatred. My own son has witnessed both of those crosses, and he has chosen that of the Savior Jesus Christ. He has chased away the Devil from this spot, and in this spot I sing your praises." Then she turned to me and said the most beautiful words I had ever heard. "You've done your daddy proud."

For a moment, it was as if I had both my parents standing beside me. I was overwhelmed with a sense of accomplishment. *I did remember the boy*, I said silently to my dad. Now the boy was a man, strong and independent. And, I promised, I won't forget the boys who depend on me. No matter what I have to do, I will not let them down.

Momma and I talked a while longer about the family and our struggles, especially the day that my two sisters and baby niece were killed by a drunk driver. She had never been able to let go of that tragic memory but managed to carry on in spite of it.

"Momma, you're a very special lady. You held us together even when our world was falling apart."

"I did what I had to do, sugar. Now help your momma into the van. I want to go see those boys."

As we neared the van, she turned and looked once more at the town, the hills, the valley, and she smiled. I knew this was both the first and last time she would ever see my mountaintop chapel.

The rest of the day, Momma visited the boys in the cabins while I attended to some work. When I entered the trailer, Carol handed me the mail with a smile. "There's some overdue bills in there." Her tone of voice was certainly different. Nothing seemed to bother her much lately. I didn't know if it was because we had weathered the storms or because the new administration building was being built.

"You know, Carol," I said as I glanced over the letters in my hand. "I think you're going to miss the trailer. I mean, this is like home."

She laughed. "Not on your life!"

When I finished my work, I found Momma sitting on the rocking chair on the porch of Cabin One. Some of the boys were gathered around her, listening to her stories about my childhood. It sure looked familiar, seeing Momma surrounded by so many children. She could touch their hearts in a second. Maybe we should hire her as a counselor . . . Naw, the state would say she didn't have enough experience.

"Okay, boys," I said, "it's almost time for dinner. Go in and get washed up. I'm going to take Momma Blount back to the farmhouse. And fellahs, don't forget, you have to sing tonight in church. White shirts and ties."

"Okay," said Henry. "But you can't sing, Mr. Mel, because you missed practice."

"What?" Momma asked. "My son missed practice? Well, we're going to have to have a talk about that." She winked at me. "Now go on, boys. We don't want to be late."

• • •

I picked the boys up at the cabins and we all drove to our local church. "They look like angels," Momma whispered to me as she watched the boys walk quietly to the front of the church. "You would be up there with them, if you hadn't missed practice."

"That's okay, Momma," I joked, "my halo's a little rusty."

Reverend Johnson talked for a while about the power of the Lord. "The Spirit moves at will," he said. "When I speak His words, I feel His power and know it must move you."

As I listened to the preacher, I watched the boys become restless. They shifted their weight from one leg to the other and began to whisper to each other. I caught the glance of one of the boys and narrowed my eyes. He stood, quiet and still. Before long, he began swaying back and forth. *Hurry up, Reverend*, I thought. I didn't know how much longer those kids could keep quiet.

He must have read my mind. "Now, ladies and gentleman," the Reverend said, "the boys from the Mel Blount Youth Home are going to sing for the Lord this evening. You all know Mr. Blount sitting over there. He's the founder of the home. He has been in the news a lot lately because he has been putting up one big fight for these boys. He's turning their souls back toward the Lord, and there's no better way to get the Lord's attention than through singing."

The Reverend stepped away from the pulpit, then leaned forward. "Oh, yes. Mr. Blount is also a former football player with the Pittsburgh Steelers. He's in the Hall of Fame, too." He looked at me apologetically, as if he had insulted me by forgetting to mention my football career.

The boys sang beautifully. As I listened, I thought my

insides were going to burst with pride. My boys were singing the Lord's praises; my momma was up for a visit; TiAnda was sitting beside me; Norris was embarking on his own challenges; the youth home was almost paying bills on time; and I was the founder first, an ex-football player second. I was feeling good.

Once my choirboys had finished, the Reverend said a benediction, then walked over to the boys and thanked them. They were indeed little angels . . . and polite, too. I could hear them introduce themselves and shake the Reverend's hand. The Reverend walked down the hall and stood by the door, wishing his parishioners a good evening.

The boys gathered around me and we began to walk out of the church. Then, as if things had been a little too heaven-like, Henry pushed Tony. "You jerk!" Tony said, loud enough to get the Reverend's attention. I knew my angels wouldn't last much longer. I grabbed both boys by an arm and escorted them down the hall.

"Goodnight, Reverend Johnson," I said, ushering the boys quickly by him. "I enjoyed your sermon."

"Goodnight, Mr. Blount," he called after me. "The boys were good."

Yes, I thought, *my boys had not only done good, they were good.*

• • •

From my mountaintop I watched as the gray clouds rushed across the sky. The harvest was over and football season had begun. I smiled at the faded memory of me, a champion from a long time ago, a black-and-gold Steeler whom I hardly recognized anymore.

The game had changed. Old records were being broken and new records were being set by the players who were now a part of the Pittsburgh Steelers. During a recent Sunday's game, one of Franco Harris's records fell to Barry Foster, a kid who runs through the defense like a hot knife cutting through butter. Chuck Noll was gone and Bill

Cowher was now the coach. Hardly a familiar face remained. The important thing, however, was that the game goes on. Somewhere I will always remain a part of it, forever fading, until I am just a name in the annals of football history.

The past several years of struggling, fighting, climbing, and crawling to keep the youth-home doors open have changed me. When God allowed me my vision, He gave me a piece of the promised land. But, like Moses, I may only get to see it from a distance.

I knew that the work that lay ahead of me would be the most difficult, but I'd be willing to go whatever distance the Lord saw fit to allow me to travel on whatever road He led me. My mind was clear. I knew what I had to do. I had to continue to push onward. I had taken steps to turn the youth home into a foundation, and I thought I'd done the right thing.

My plan was to start another youth home, then another, and I wouldn't stop until the Lord sent for me. I knew in my heart that I had to pull away from the state funding and the local child-youth services. It was clear that they had other plans for the youth home that did not include me. Therefore, I intended to open youth homes in other states and offer shelter to boys referred to us from private organizations and churches. I would rather save one child than lose twenty-four.

I was certain, once I put my plan into action, that there might be times that I would be able to help only one child. But right now, I was losing twenty to the ignorance of the powers that be.

The decision had been difficult and could prove dangerous, for I knew I would have tougher, harsher critics watching my every move.

Lord, help me find a way to free my home of its debts, I prayed. *And send me children that I can help.*

"I am your servant, Lord," I called to the trees, the hills, the grass underfoot. "I am but a branch, and you are the mighty tree."

Suddenly, I heard the cry of a hawk and looked up into the sky. A redtailed hawk circled the field, then swooped down, trapped a field mouse in its talons and soared back into the air. I watched as the hawk and its prey disappeared into the woods.

"So, Lord," I whispered, *"has my struggle only begun?"*

I already knew the answer. But everything was all right with me, for now I better understood the message of the Cross. The Klan had actually driven the meaning home to me. When they used the cross as a symbol of hatred and ignorance, I realized that I must use the cross that burns brightly within me to serve as a witness to God's grace and love for all of us.

This in itself is not easy to do. Christians risk ridicule daily for living their faith. We are the last group of people who are not protected by "political correctness." We must endure the desecration of our holy symbol because of another group's or person's right to freedom of speech and expression. It sometimes seems, however, that the cross is the only religious symbol that's not protected from this treatment.

The faith of Christians will continue. Of this I remain confident. This Christian, Mel Blount, is proud to take the hand of the Lord and walk with Him. I will never hesitate to look anyone in the eye and say, "I am a believer!"

Co-Author's Note

S H O R T L Y after the article and editorial appeared on Mel Blount, the Pittsburgh newspaper entered into a dispute with one of its labor unions. The union went on strike. Approximately six months later, the paper was sold. At this writing, Pittsburgh was without a newspaper.

The Department of Public Welfare downgraded the license of the youth home. Although Mel Blount was not notified by the department of their decision to do so, the Department of Public Welfare did notify the local media. The local media were the ones who notified the youth home.

The local zoning board granted approval to increase the number of children allowed at the home. They denied extending the age limit.

The youth home is awaiting approval for its permanent license to be extended. The decision from the Department of Public Welfare will be forthcoming two days after Christmas.

Mel Blount has been named recipient of the National Caring Award and will be inducted into the Hall of Fame for Caring Americans in Washington, D.C.

Mel Blount is now in the process of setting up a foundation that will enable him to establish youth homes nationwide.

The events in this book are based upon true incidents. Some names have been changed to protect the identities of individuals. For dramatic purposes, the chronology of some events has been compressed or altered. The intent of this story is neither to glorify nor condemn those involved but to show how, through the grace of God, a person can grow, not only by accepting support but also by facing opposition.